The
ASTROLOGICAL GUIDE
to
SEDUCTION AND ROMANCE

The
ASTROLOGICAL GUIDE
to
SEDUCTION AND ROMANCE

How to Love a Libra,
Turn On a Taurus,
and Seduce a Sagittarius

Susan Sheppard

A Citadel Press Book
Published by Carol Publishing Group

A Citadel Press Book
Published by Carol Publishing Group
Citadel Press is a registered trademark of Carol Communications, Inc.

Editorial, sales and distribution, and rights and permissions inquiries should be
addressed to Carol Publishing Group, 120 Enterprise Avenue, Secaucus, N.J.
07094.

In Canada: Canadian Manda Group, One Atlantic Avenue, Suite 105, Toronto,
Ontario M6K 3E7

Manufactured in the United States of America
ISBN 0-7394-0430-X

CONTENTS

Preface   vii
Introduction   xi

PREFACE

Whatever is born or done in a moment of time, has the qualities of this moment in time. . . .

—CARL GUSTAV JUNG

The practice of astrology is probably the oldest science and the second oldest profession in the world. As human beings, we have always sensed that we are taking part in some higher order, that we all have a destiny to fulfill, and that destiny has been with us since birth.

This belief is held by many people, including those who do not believe in astrology. Most of us, however, have faith in some greater plan for our lives. Perhaps we find purpose in our religion. Others might discover their destinies through the higher realities of science, while others work out their fate through romantic attractions, connections with people, or humanitarian causes. Depending upon your perspective, this understanding of a greater plan can create comfort or high anxiety. Astrology promises that we can understand and take part in our own fate, or it can point out areas where we tend to lose control.

Some of the areas of most anxiety in our lives pertain to romance, intimacy, and sex. In these areas most of us feel quite vulnerable. After all, in order to enjoy life to its fullest, we must have connection with others, through the interrelation of family and friends, or the interrelation of romance and sex. Normally, our friends and family accept us for who we are. We hope this is the case with our romantic partners as well; but romance is complicated by sex, the greatest form of intimacy among humans.

When we enter a new romance, we often come to the relationship in ignorance, trusting that the slight information we have about our prospective lover is accurate, when in truth, we know him or her only superficially. By understanding the fundamentals of astrology and casting your lover's horoscope, you can come to the love relationship with more knowledge and influence than most lovers have. It's as if you have read an in-depth analysis of your lover, observed by an ancient genius schooled in the marvels and mysteries of human nature.

In my years as an astrologer, I have learned one basic truth. Astrology never lies about a person. Once you've studied a birth chart, you pretty much know what your subject is all about. There may be some surprises. Perhaps my client is a little more or less spiritual than I expected. Perhaps my subject has chosen not to push himself in terms of his talent and ability, while others less talented will give it all they have, and end up surprising successes. Nevertheless, the astrologer can clearly see how introverted or extroverted her subjects are. She can see what they desire sexually and what sexual angels or demons drive them. The astrologer can see how deeply her subjects feel, how empathic they are, or how emotionally removed they are. The astrologer can ascertain how cunning her clients are or how naive they might be. The astrologer can also clearly see what the natal chart reveals in terms of love, attraction, and sex.

Perhaps if people realized what stunning information their natal horoscopes reveal, akin to a private history or a secret confession, they would give out their birth dates less freely. After all, in doing so, they are baring their immortal souls.

Understanding astrology does not give you power, but it gives you greater insight. Such insight can be used for your benefit, especially in those complicated matters of romance, seduction, and sexual attraction. In order to have a great love in your life, you must also have great wisdom and understanding. This can be achieved simply by comprehending the most fundamental elements of astrology, such as Sun signs, Venus and Mars signs, Saturn signs, and Rising signs that will be discussed in this book. Herein lies the wisdom to make love yours.

Once you use the power of the stars and their signs, you can provide that understanding, not only for your lover, but also for yourself. You will realize why you were born to be together. In finding your love, not even the sky is the limit.

INTRODUCTION

When it comes to romance and seduction, understanding Sun signs (the sign used in popular horoscopes found in newspapers and magazines) is simply not enough. Your "sign" is only one small fragment of all the information your natal chart holds. Although the Sun sign certainly reveals the "outer person," or personality that other people see, the Sun is probably the least complex element in your horoscope and means very little as far as sexual and romantic compatibility are concerned.

In the natal horoscope (birth chart), specific areas reveal our romantic and sexual needs. A trained astrologer can easily determine, when looking at a natal chart, whether her client has the tendency to be bisexual or gay. She can see other sexual preferences as well. (Scary, isn't it?) The fact of the matter is, our natal charts show us on a deep level what it takes to make our lovers and ourselves emotionally and sexually satisfied. One might even conclude that the stars know us better than we know ourselves.

Although the natal, or "birth," chart takes years to fully comprehend, certain basics will enable you to find out what makes you and your lover tick, not to mention what turns you both on. For romance and seduction, we turn to the Rising signs, representing not only our egos, but our "other" self and "lover" self. (This may explain why some people marry the lover who looks like them the most.) In this book, we will look at the compatibility of Venus and Mars signs, our favorite planet lovers who frolic among the stars. Also covered are Saturn signs, the planet of time and measure, of destiny and karma. After all, what would love be without karma? In addition, we will briefly study the Houses (i.e., the twelve divisions of the heavens, each of which is assigned a zodiac sign and signifies an aspect of yourself or your environment) that are most conducive to romance becoming a permanent fixture in your life. Do you know what House your lover lives in? Read on to learn some basics when it comes to the astrology of love and sex.

WHAT IS A NATAL CHART?

Your natal chart is simply a snapshot of the way the sky looked at the exact moment you were born. It charts the courses of all of the planets, not just your Sun sign.

We read about our Sun signs and we understand that this correlates to the hour, day, month, and time of year in which we are born, but we have other signs as well. The planets and their signs are constantly changing, because planets move through the various signs on different time schedules. Whereas the Sun moves into a different sign every month, the Moon moves through a different sign every two and a half days. Yet the planet Pluto can take from thirteen to thirty-two years to move through a sign. In this book we will concentrate on the planets of love, sex, and karma and those are Venus, Mars, and Saturn, respectively.

You will be given charts to help you determine your Venus, Mars, and Rising signs. They are the most important signs when it comes to sex and romance. In order to look at your own natal chart in depth, you need to have your natal chart cast. There are several sites on the Internet that will cast your horoscope for free as long as you have your date, time, and place of birth. For now, you can use the simple guides in this book to find your Venus, Mars, and Rising signs, as well as your lover's.

WHAT IS A RISING SIGN?

I'm sure you know of the star groups called constellations. Since ancient times, humankind has used twelve of these star groups, or constellations, to make up the zodiac. Ancient peoples attributed human and animal characteristics to the signs, such as Virgo the Virgin, Cancer the Crab, and Scorpio the Scorpion. Every day, the Earth passes through all twelve signs. So, at the moment you were born, one of the astrological constellations was "rising," or moving up over the eastern horizon. This is what we call the "Rising sign." It takes the Earth about two hours to pass by one of the Houses, or signs. Thus, in twenty-four hours, the Earth passes through all of the twelve signs. The hour you were born determines your Rising sign.

For instance, if you are a Cancer born about 8:30 A.M., your Rising sign would be Leo. If you are a Cancer born about 10:00 A.M., however, then your Rising sign would be Virgo, the next sign in line. If you were born under a different sign, it changes. For example, if you were born in mid-December at daybreak, your Rising sign would be the same as your Sun sign, which would be Sagittarius, but if you were born two hours after daybreak, then your Rising sign would be the next sign: Capricorn. Add two more hours, and your Rising sign would be Aquarius.

Got the picture? No? An easy way to ascertain Rising signs can be rather simple, unless you were born around the time the signs change. The Rising sign is the same as the Sun sign at precisely daybreak. Therefore, you can easily deduce your Rising sign, but if you're still confused over it, a simple table of Rising signs is in Chapter Six, "The Rising Sign and Romance." All you have to do is run your finger down the page and locate your sign and time of birth. Presto—there's your Rising sign—plain and simple. (Please make adjustments for Daylight Savings Time.)

PLANETS: YOU ARE MUCH MORE THAN YOUR SUN SIGN

Over the years many people have argued whether astrology is a science or an art. It is actually a little of both. If astrology is an art, then it is a very complicated art, because it takes a good amount of mathematical and scientific ability to cast a natal chart, not to mention astrological forecasts.

To begin with, you are much more than your Sun sign. In every natal chart, you also have a Moon sign, Mercury sign, Venus sign, Mars sign, Jupiter sign, Saturn sign, Uranus sign, Neptune sign, and Pluto sign, not to mention the Rising sign. The eight planets and two luminaries (the Sun and Moon) fall in the various signs at the time you were born. It is very unlikely that they are all in the same sign. For instance, you may have your Sun in carefree Sagittarius, while your Venus and Mars fall in passionate, possessive Scorpio. As a result, you are probably more possessive than a typical Sagittarian would be.

In this book, we only concentrate on the signs that have the most influence on romance—your Sun, Venus, Mars, Saturn, and Rising signs. These planets are the most significant when it comes to romance, as they govern certain laws of attraction between the sexes. After you become familiar with your own natal chart, however, you will find that other planets, such as Neptune and Uranus, also play a part, although not as directly.

In this book, let's stick to the basics of Venus and Mars, the planets of love and sex, as well as your Sun and Saturn signs, covering your natal planets of personality and fated relationships. The Rising sign shows what type of individual we tend to be attracted to and what kind of lover we must have to fulfill our most basic needs. Once you understand the basics of your Rising sign, you will learn what to look for and what to expect in the mate who is perfect for you.

So where does one get information on the planets and their signs? It's very simple. You buy a world ephemeris for the twentieth and the twenty-first centuries. Many publishers print such books; it can be ordered from your local bookstore or over the Internet. The one I use is the *World Ephemeris for the Twentieth Century 1900 to 2000 at Midnight*, published by Para Research, with a preface by Robert Hand. Pages xvi–xvii shows an example of two months.

As you can see, an ephemeris is very simple to read. The degrees and signs of the planets are listed as they appear at midnight. Here are the planets in their signs during November and December of 2000.

Notice that the Moon moves rather quickly—from one sign into another every two and a half days. Pluto, however, can stay in a sign for as long as thirty years.

NOVEMBER 2000

Day	Sid. T.	Sun	Moon	Merc.	Venus	Mars	Jup.	Saturn	Uranus	Nept.	Pluto	N.Node
1	2:42:21	8Sc52 9	2Cp59	4Sc34R	15Sg26	28Vi 6	9Ge31R	28Ta57R	16Aq54	3Aq52	11Sg30	18Cn55
2	2:46:17	9 52 13	14 54	3 26	16 38	28 43	9 25	28 53	16 55	3 53	11 32	18 52
3	2:50:13	10 52 18	26 43	2 25	17 51	29 20	9 19	28 48	16 55	3 53	11 35	18 49
4	2:54:10	11 52 25	8Aq31	1 33	19 3	29 57	9 12	28 44	16 55	3 54	11 37	18 46
5	2:58: 6	12 52 33	20 23	0 52	20 16	0Li34	9 6	28 39	16 56	3 55	11 39	18 42
6	3: 2: 3	13 52 43	2Pi25	0 22	21 28	1 11	8 59	28 34	16 56	3 55	11 41	18 39
7	3: 6: 0	14 52 55	14 42	29L156	22 40	1 48	8 52	28 30	16 57	3 56	11 43	18 36
8	3: 9:57	15 53 8	27 18	0Sc 1D	23 53	2 25	8 45	28 25	16 57	3 57	11 45	18 33
9	3:13:53	16 53 22	10Ar17	0 16	25 5	3 2	8 38	28 20	16 58	3 58	11 47	18 30
10	3:17:49	17 53 38	23 38	0 41	26 17	3 38	8 31	28 16	16 59	3 58	11 49	18 27
11	3:21:46	18 53 56	7Ta22	1 15	27 29	4 15	8 24	28 11	17 0	3 59	11 51	18 23
12	3:25:42	19 54 15	21 25	1 58	28 41	4 52	8 16	28 6	17 0	4 0	11 54	18 20
13	3:29:39	20 54 36	5Ge42	2 47	29 53	5 29	8 9	28 1	17 1	4 1	11 56	18 17
14	3:33:36	21 54 59	20 4	3 43	1Cp 5	6 6	8 1	27 56	17 2	4 2	11 58	18 14
15	3:37:33	22 55 24	4Cn37	4 45	2 17	6 42	7 54	27 52	17 3	4 3	12 0	18 11
16	3:41:29	23 55 50	19 4	5 52	3 29	7 19	7 46	27 47	17 4	4 4	12 3	18 7
17	3:45:25	24 56 19	3Le23	7 3	4 41	7 56	7 38	27 42	17 5	4 5	12 5	18 4
18	3:49:22	25 56 49	17 34	8 17	5 53	8 33	7 30	27 37	17 6	4 6	12 7	18 1
19	3:53:18	26 57 21	1Vi35	9 35	7 4	9 9	7 22	27 32	17 7	4 7	12 9	17 58
20	3:57:15	27 57 55	15 26	10 55	8 16	9 46	7 14	27 27	17 9	4 9	12 12	17 55
21	4: 1:12	28 58 30	29 8	12 18	9 28	10 23	7 6	27 22	17 10	4 10	12 14	17 52
22	4: 5: 8	29 59 7	12L135	13 42	10 39	10 59	6 58	27 17	17 12	4 12	12 16	17 48
23	4: 9: 4	0Sg59 46	25 52	15 8	11 51	11 36	6 50	27 13	17 13	4 13	12 18	17 45
24	4:13: 1	2 0 27	8Sc56	16 36	13 3	12 12	6 42	27 8	17 14	4 15	12 21	17 42
25	4:16:58	3 1 9	21 47	18 4	14 14	12 49	6 34	27 3	17 16	4 16	12 23	17 39
26	4:20:54	4 1 53	4Sg25	19 33	15 25	13 25	6 26	26 58	17 17	4 16	12 25	17 36
27	4:24:51	5 2 37	16 49	21 3	16 36	14 2	6 17	26 53	17 18	4 17	12 28	17 33
28	4:28:48	6 3 24	29 1	22 34	17 47	14 38	6 9	26 48	17 20	4 19	12 30	17 29
29	4:32:44	7 4 11	11Cp 1	24 5	18 58	15 15	6 1	26 44	17 21	4 20	12 32	17 26
30	4:36:40	8 4 59	22 54	25 37	20 9	15 51	5 53	26 39	17 23	4 22	12 35	17 23

11/22 Sun in Sag. 0:21   11/4 1st Qt. 7:28   11/11 Full 21:16   11/18 3rd Qt. 15:26   11/25 New 23:12

xvi

DECEMBER 2000

Day	Sid. T.	Sun	Moon	Merc.	Venus	Mars	Jup.	Saturn	Uranus	Nept.	Pluto	N.Node
1	4:40:37	9Sg 5 49	4Aq41	25Sc37	21Cp20	16Li27	5Ge45R	26Ta34R	17Aq25	4Aq23	12Sg37	17Cn20
2	4:44:34	10 6 39	16 28	27 9	22 31	17 4	5 36	26 29	17 27	4 25	12 39	17 17
3	4:48:30	11 7 30	28 19	28 41	23 42	17 40	5 28	26 25	17 29	4 26	12 42	17 13
4	4:52:27	12 8 23	10Pi19	0Sg14	24 53	18 16	5 20	26 20	17 31	4 28	12 44	17 10
5	4:56:24	13 9 15	22 34	1 46	26 3	18 52	5 12	26 16	17 34	4 29	12 46	17 7
6	5: 0:20	14 10 9	5Ar 7	3 19	27 14	19 29	5 4	26 11	17 36	4 31	12 48	17 4
7	5: 4:16	15 11 4	18 4	4 52	28 24	20 5	4 56	26 7	17 38	4 32	12 51	17 1
8	5: 8:13	16 11 59	1Ta26	6 25	29 34	20 41	4 48	26 2	17 41	4 34	12 53	16 58
9	5:12: 9	17 12 55	15 16	7 58	0Aq44	21 17	4 41	25 58	17 43	4 36	12 55	16 54
10	5:16: 6	18 13 52	29 29	9 31	1 54	21 53	4 33	25 53	17 45	4 37	12 58	16 51
11	5:20: 3	19 14 49	14Ge 4	11 4	3 4	22 29	4 25	25 49	17 47	4 39	13 0	16 48
12	5:23:59	20 15 48	28 52	12 38	4 14	23 5	4 18	25 45	17 49	4 41	13 2	16 45
13	5:27:56	21 16 47	13Cn47	14 11	5 24	23 41	4 10	25 41	17 52	4 43	13 5	16 42
14	5:31:52	22 17 47	28 40	15 45	6 33	24 17	4 3	25 37	17 54	4 44	13 7	16 39
15	5:35:49	23 18 48	13Le24	17 18	7 43	24 53	3 55	25 33	17 56	4 46	13 9	16 35
16	5:39:45	24 19 50	27 54	18 52	8 52	25 28	3 48	25 29	17 59	4 48	13 12	16 32
17	5:43:42	25 20 54	12Vi 7	20 26	10 1	26 4	3 41	25 25	18 1	4 50	13 14	16 29
18	5:47:39	26 21 57	26 4	22 0	11 10	26 40	3 34	25 21	18 4	4 52	13 16	16 26
19	5:51:35	27 23 2	9Li34	23 34	12 19	27 16	3 27	25 17	18 6	4 54	13 18	16 23
20	5:55:32	28 24 8	22 49	25 8	13 28	27 51	3 21	25 13	18 9	4 56	13 21	16 19
21	5:59:28	29 25 15	5Sc48	26 42	14 36	28 27	3 14	25 10	18 11	4 57	13 23	16 16
22	6: 3:25	0Cp26 22	18 3	28 17	15 44	29 2	3 7	25 6	18 14	4 59	13 25	16 13
23	6: 7:21	1 27 30	1Sg 3	29 52	16 52	29 38	3 1	25 3	18 16	5 1	13 27	16 10
24	6:11:18	2 28 38	13 23	1Cp27	18 0	0Sc14	2 55	24 59	18 19	5 3	13 30	16 7
25	6:15:14	3 29 47	25 32	3 2	19 9	0 49	2 49	24 56	18 22	5 5	13 32	16 4
26	6:19:11	4 30 57	7Cp33	4 38	20 16	1 25	2 43	24 53	18 25	5 7	13 34	16 0
27	6:23: 8	5 32 8	19 27	6 13	21 24	2 0	2 37	24 50	18 27	5 9	13 36	15 57
28	6:27: 4	6 33 18	1Aq16	7 49	22 31	2 35	2 32	24 47	18 30	5 11	13 39	15 54
29	6:31: 1	7 34 29	13 3	9 26	23 38	3 11	2 26	24 44	18 33	5 14	13 41	15 51
30	6:34:57	8 35 39	24 51	11 2	24 45	3 46	2 21	24 41	18 33	5 16	13 43	15 48
31	6:38:54	9 36 47	6Pi42	12 39	25 52	4 21	2 16	24 38	18 36	5 18	13 45	15 45

12/21 Sun in Cap. 13:39   12/4 1st Qt. 3:56   12/11 Full 9:04   12/18 3rd Qt. 0:43   12/25 New 17:23(E)

HOUSES

What in heaven's name are "Houses" and why in hell are they here? I asked myself this question many times when learning astrology long, long ago. Houses, in effect, are where the zodiac's constellations live. Really, the astrological houses are divisions or boundaries thought up by humankind. The Houses are used to give some order to the zodiac. The Houses help divide the differences in our minds. In order to understand something, man must impose his order upon it. This is true of all sciences, and, of course, it is true of astrology.

There are twelve houses to the zodiac. Our modern zodiac is typically the Greek/Babylonian version. (So if you find yourself throwing up your hands while reading this book and cursing, "It's all Greek to me!" then you are correct, Keemosabe!) Western astrologers (which we are) use the Greek/Babylonian method, which has twelve houses. It's as simple as that. The sky is divided into twelve sections like a pizza pie. These twelve sections make up the twelve astrological Houses. Your Rising sign makes up your First House. The First House is the House of Self, of outward personality and outward appearance. The First House is what we have that "attracts." It even rules our scent. Therefore, the opposite house, which is the Seventh House of Partners, is the type we find attractive or attracted to us.

Certain astrological Houses govern romance and sex more than the others do. These "love" Houses are generally considered to be the Fifth House of Love and Pleasure (governing romantic love), the Seventh House of Marriage and Partners (governing long-term partners), the Eighth House of Mystery and Sex (governing sexual attraction and sexual love), and the Eleventh House of Friends and Associates (governing brotherly love). Most important in the law of attraction is your Rising sign/First House. (They are the same.)

You needn't worry about these Houses yet. Just worry about getting your Rising sign correct. For instance, if you find that your Rising sign is Leo, and your lover has many planets in Leo, you can be assured the attraction is substantial and very real.

Before delving into the planets and their houses, let's master some basics of astrology. That is: what you thought you knew about your Sun sign and your lover's, but probably didn't.

The
ASTROLOGICAL GUIDE
to
SEDUCTION AND ROMANCE

ONE

THE SECRET
OF THE SIGNS:
WHAT YOU PROBABLY
DIDN'T KNOW

If you've read up on the Sun signs, you probably don't expect too many surprises in this book. You may only be looking for an affirmation of information of which you are already aware. If you've studied astrology for a number of years, however, you will come to see that certain traits and attributes of the signs are not readily apparent. Astrologers see the outer person, and sense some of the inner person, but there is an even deeper core to each person to be discovered through his or her astrological sign. Sometimes it is more flattering than is commonly known about each sign's shared traits—and often, much less flattering than what is commonly known.

In the following descriptions, I have shed further light on the twelve signs. Read on and see a part of your lover that you may not have learned about from mainstream astrology books. There may be some surprises. Use them to your benefit—in romance and in life.

ARIES (MARCH 21–APRIL 19)

An often overlooked side to Aries is his inordinate sensitivity. Most astrology books turn Aries the Ram into a fire-breathing devil. After all, Aries is Mars-ruled, meaning he is governed by the god of war. Such a reputation is hard to live down. In fact, Aries is a sign of enormous aggression, and he can choose to use this aggression in either positive or negative ways. Aries is confrontational and has difficulty being any other way. It is only natural that we all have come to assume that Aries is a brute best to be avoided, but did you know that Aries is as superbly sensitive as a Cancer? Aries just refuses to show it since he doesn't want to appear weak or off his guard. The sign of the Ram is sensitive about the way others view him, and in his view, it seems that people are always picking on him for no apparent reason. Push his most sensitive buttons and Aries quickly flares up. Such rawness of emotion can be shocking, if not alarming, to those closest to him. Aries' sensitivity isolates him, keeping both friends and lovers at bay. Because Aries is often agitated, others avoid him, turning him into a loner with only his own thoughts for company. As an elevated thinker, Aries is a poet in his soul, but because he is always fighting, the poetic aspect dies early and his role as a warrior dominates. Awaken the poet in Aries and you will touch the sensitive parts few others have ever reached.

Element: Fire
Planet: Mars
Best Trait: Energy with imagination
Worst Trait: Senseless cruelty

TAURUS (APRIL 20–MAY 20)

A little-known aspect of Taurus is the intensity of his sexual appetite. Recently, it has been said that Taurus is the horniest sign in the entire zodiac. This bull-necked rocket of testosterone can't get enough sex, and that's a fact not usually discussed in mainstream astrology books. In print, sexual intensity is all given over to Scorpio, which tends to be highly exaggerated. Taurus, however, is the one with the most sexual drive. After all, he is an Earth sign, very much aware of the needs of the physical body. Whatever is seen, tasted, or felt means the most to a Taurus. Forget about that connection-between-two-souls thing. Taurus prefers sweat over spirit. When it comes to heads or tails, Taurus prefers the tail. You must keep in mind that Taurus is the sign of the appetite and he is also Venus-ruled, a sign of both edible and sensual pleasures.

Scorpio has periods of sexual excess for which he is famous, but Taurus is just all-around horny, and he'll bed just about anyone because it's all about satisfying his appetite, not a power thing as it is with Scorpio. Taurus is so calm and relaxed that it doesn't seem unnatural to spend all day in the bedroom, luxuriating between the sheets and worshiping each other's bodies. Taurus is placid but has a mounting desire. The best flame for Taurus is one of sustained sexual fire, and that flame comes out of solid Earth, but that's not all that's solid about your Taurus! Bon appétit and hit the sheets!

Element: Earth
Planet: Venus
Best Trait: Loyalty
Worst Trait: Staying perversely obstinate

GEMINI (MAY 21–JUNE 20)

A somewhat inconspicuous characteristic of Geminis is that they are much smarter than they act. In fact, Geminis are often overlooked geniuses. You cannot, however, get them to stop talking no matter what you do. This is their way of controlling a situation, by filling up the atmosphere with words that are seldom pertinent to the conversation. What Geminis should do is practice some verbal restraint and learn to cultivate a sense of mystery about themselves. Incessant talking gets in the way of a Gemini's happiness. Talking creates a space between him and other people. Geminis tend not to listen very well either, and this is why they get most of their information from television and books. The Twins can't be still long enough to learn from others. Thus, they often flunk out of college despite glowing recommendations and impressive term papers. It's lucky that Geminis are uncommonly intelligent, but this is often overshadowed by their endless prattle about nothing in particular.

The other secret is that Geminis suffer from bad nerves and conflicting emotions. They are often agitated because they are in an endless cycle of trying to explain themselves to others, hoping to be understood, yet no one seems to understand them. Geminis are flattered when you take seriously what they have to say. You should teach Geminis how to ask questions, too. This would ensure them the popularity and respect they long for. Give your Gemini respect and remind him when it's time to stop talking.

Element: Air
Planet: Mercury
Best Trait: A curious and magnificent mind
Worst Trait: Becoming an impossible bore

CANCER (JUNE 20–JULY 22)

People born under the sign of Cancer are also known as Moon children because their planetary sign is the Moon. Before you assume that a Cancer is a soft touch, keep in mind that Cancer is actually a rather contrary and controlling water sign. Cancerian individuals have great feeling and compassion, but they can also be snitty and insist that things go only their way. If you don't comply with the wishes of a Cancer, you will indeed be made to suffer. No one can be quite as crabby as a Cancer.

The sign of the Crab is also insanely tenacious. Cancer people will pinch your heart with their claws and then never let go unless you rip yourself away, ripping your heart in the process. Males born under the sign of Cancer have doubts about their masculinity, secretly fearing they are gay because, after all, Cancer is a feminine sign, meaning their reactions are ones of great emotion. So Cancer is the sign that gets sand kicked in his face at the beach, but when he grows up to be bigger and stronger than anyone ever imagined, watch out! Cancers will get revenge, not necessarily in a cruel way, but in a very precise way, letting you know how you have hurt them! Of course, many of the hurts are highly embellished and imagined. You don't have to do much to Cancers to make them mad as a hornet. Keep in mind, Cancers are sensitive and under those hard shells beat tender hearts. But you will only get Cancers' love once they decide that you truly, truly deserve it—and not a minute before.

Element: Water
Planet: The Moon
Best Trait: Waves and waves of compassion
Worst Trait: Becoming highly irritated over trivial matters

LEO (JULY 23–AUGUST 22)

Leo wants to be a star but secretly believes he doesn't deserve any special recognition. In his eyes, everyone else is more worthy of the stardom. In his own eyes, Leo is just an imposter—someone who pretends to be something that he is not: a person who is great, for instance. At least, this is what he fears. Leo is also plagued by worries that he is ugly or somehow unattractive. Preening and posing before mirrors, and the need for attention that Leo is so famous for, are actually symbols of his deep insecurity. Some signs, such as Cancer and Virgo, are known for their insecurities, but Leo is thought to be bold and proud, which he is.

Leo, however, has caused a problem for himself. He wants to impress and be admired so much that he must always be "one-up" on everyone else. Leo must be the best. Leo can't just "measure up" like the rest of us and be one among the crowd—he must always be the leader, the star worshiped from afar. We can only imagine how lonely this must be. Because Leo *is* often very impressive, we fail to see the isolation of his throne where he typically governs alone. Leo can overcome this loneliness and isolation by becoming truly intimate with someone, but in order to do this, Leo must let go of his ego and allow his true soul to shine through like the Sun. In doing this, he will see (and so will others) that he is truly beautiful without the props and traps of fame and glory that he often surrounds himself with.

Element: Fire
Planet: The Sun
Best Trait: A true original
Worst Trait: A vainglorious fraud

VIRGO (AUGUST 23–SEPTEMBER 22)

Virgo is plagued by invasive thoughts that he cannot control. Often these thoughts have to do with his hidden aggressions and sexual impulses, and Virgo secretly fears he will act upon them. At the same time, Virgo also fears that such thoughts will turn even more perverted or twisted and, even worse, that people can read his mind. This is why most people born under the sign of Virgo are afraid to visit psychics. Virgos believe that guilt and sin are written all over them. No one can measure up to their rules of perfectionism, most especially themselves.

The fact of the matter is, Virgo worries about things that aren't even real. Try to convince Virgo that everyone has occasional weird thoughts, and Virgo will assure you that none can be as bad as his. Tell Virgo that no one is perfect (not even him) and Virgo will say that his mother is. One would have difficulty running into a Virgo without a conscience. Virgo is a very guilt-stricken sign.

He is critical of others in order to cover up his own faults and flaws. It's so much easier to wag a finger at someone else. Virgo's perfectionism is vigilant and enslaving. Those born under this sign require relief and reassurance. They also need forgiveness. Therefore, in love, Virgo is looking for someone who can forgive him of all of his awful traits. Other than the faultfinding and the petty criticisms, the rest of us can't see them, of course.

Element: Earth
Planet: Mercury
Best Trait: Reliability
Worst Trait: Torturous criticism

LIBRA (SEPTEMBER 23–OCTOBER 22)

This sign is sooooo easy. Often drop-dead gorgeous, Libra loves nothing better than to give love. Libra also attracts wealth, gifts, and possessions, but did you know that Libra is a moocher? The sign of the Scales is a strange combination of aggressive and passive energies. Charming and at ease with others, Libra can also be quite pushy about starting up a relationship. After all, Libra does not feel alive unless he has someone dangling off his elbow (or from some other place).

After initiating the affair and playing the Prince or Princess of your dreams, Libra turns the tables and wants you to take care of everything. Libra then takes this to the extreme by becoming a serious moocher, the kind that goes around living off others. Librans seldom own their own stuff. It either is on credit, is borrowed from family members, or belongs to friends. Libra is famous for running businesses out of hotel rooms or eking out a living house-sitting.

After you meet Libra, he is probably already dreaming of ways he can move in with you. This is a sign that has trouble going it alone. Hell to a Libra is being without friends and connections. Librans wish to be pampered and want the good things in life to be brought to them and placed at their feet on a velvet pillow. Libra needs you and needs associations. In love, Libra is happy just to have a partner. Work as companions or coconspirators and Libra will stay yours forever.

Element: Air
Planet: Venus
Best Traits: Charm and creativity
Worst Traits: Forcing love, being swinish and manipulative

SCORPIO (OCTOBER 23–NOVEMBER 21)

If the zodiac has a sign of legend, it is certainly Scorpio. What other sign is such a master of influence and control? The real truth is, Scorpio secretly fears that he is a wuss who is about to be put upon by everyone. This is what causes Scorpio to have some problems in the area of openness and generosity. If you feel that something is about to be taken away, you won't feel too generous, now will you? Scorpio is a sign that feels some lack. He fears he will turn weak or become somehow out-of-control and everything that he has worked so hard for will go to hell in a handbasket.

Since he is a Water sign, Scorpio is deeply emotional and capable of great empathy. At his best, Scorpio is inordinately loving and giving. It's just that Scorpio views this as a weakness rather than a strength. Scorpio remembers his childhood and how the other kids always ganged up on him. He also remembers how he got blamed for things that he didn't do, and he is still bitter about it. Scorpio often overcompensates by turning cold-hearted. Scorpio's perceived lack of sympathy by lovers is the root of his difficulties in romantic relationships. Scorpio often believes others are controlling him, when in truth it is Scorpio doing the manipulating. Cultivating intimacy and trust is the best way to relax the overpowering impulse Scorpio has to control. The more Scorpio learns to trust, the more of a softy he becomes.

Element: Water
Planet: Pluto
Best Trait: Focus
Worst Trait: Cruelty

SAGITTARIUS (NOVEMBER 22–DECEMBER 21)

Who doesn't understand good ol' Sag? Actually, none of us do. The typical Sagittarius has cultivated a friendly, clown exterior but it's not really him. He is far more complicated than he appears. The sign of the Archer is such a gambler that he will gamble his life away in the bat of an eye. The one thing Sagittarians can't stand is boredom, and most especially, intellectual boredom. They'll do anything to avoid it, even put themselves in the worst positions possible because of it. Life is an opportunistic game to Sagittarius.

He is a rebel but knows he must obey the rules of some higher authority to make his plans work. For this reason, Sagittarius can often become a closet religious fiend. Youthful manifestations of rebellion such as wearing black leather, chains, and jeans, can incredibly become Sag in a three-piece suit. It's even harder imagining Sagittarius going to church, but such is often the case. Early rebellion with dirt biking and bar brawling often turns into a fascination with religion and all of its pomp and circumstance. So in order to get along with the Sagittarius in a romantic way, it is of utmost importance to "hear" his ideas while Sag ponders the subject of why we are here on this ball of dirt called Earth. In love, allow Sagittarius to become the hero he truly is at heart. You'll find that his gambling and playing the field gets less intense. Perhaps his hair-brained philosophies will even make sense.

Element: Fire
Planet: Jupiter
Best Trait: Truthfulness
Worst Trait: Truthfulness

CAPRICORN (DECEMBER 22–JANUARY 19)

He's rough. He's tough. So what can you expect from Billy Goat Gruff? Capricorn says everyone must play by all the rules, and he gets awfully dour if we don't. Capricorn's secret is that he fears he will lose control and get easily carried away, showing a complete lack of judgment. Capricorn tries to use his informed judgment in relationships, but often shoots himself in the foot.

The problem is, Capricorn goes for the partner whom he believes "measures up" to his standards, meaning someone he believes has a good job, old money, or influential family connections. He goes for the partner whom he believes is rich, and guess what? The person may be rich but may also turn out to be a raving lunatic or something as boring and colorless as a bag of sand. Then Capricorn has to wonder, "Was it worth the influence and the power getting hooked up with some ball and chain?" Perhaps not. So that relationship dissolves, but Capricorn doesn't give up. Why no, Cap doesn't even know the meaning of the word *quit*. So off he goes chasing Ms. Moneybags again—and the band plays on.

Another irritating trait many Capricorns have is they will give you something and then ask for it back, completely forgetting any favors you've done for them. So what does Capricorn need to know in finding a lover? Capricorn should give his lover time to develop. Capricorn also needs to know that marrying power and influence doesn't necessarily ensure the same for him. Capricorn should remember that his best lover is the one who keeps caring.

Element: Earth
Planet: Saturn
Best Trait: Common sense
Worst Trait: Gluttony

AQUARIUS (JANUARY 20–FEBRUARY 18)

Have you ever been romanced by an alien from outer space? Well, that's what it's like to be loved by an Aquarius. Despite all of the far-out antics and ideas, though, Aquarius is really a closet conservative. Many Aquarians actually believe in the very rules they feel so very compelled to break. Just like their opposite sign, Leo, Aquarians fancy themselves extremely special. They don't want to contradict this belief by going along with the status quo or the powers that be. After all, the original planetary ruler of Aquarius was Saturn, planet of cause and effect, and planet of the law.

The typical Aquarius is eager to embrace the new and different, but he can also reject these ideas and actions just as easily. The more you get to know your Aquarian lover, the more you will see the self-discipline and covered-up conservatism. The social ideas of the Aquarius tend to go to the extreme. If you don't believe this, just remember that Aquarian President Ronald Reagan was a far-out liberal in his early days in Hollywood.

No matter what his stance, Aquarius is the sign that moves against the tides. If life is boring, Aquarius makes things *interesting* by pushing all kinds of buzzers and buttons that stir up members of polite society. This is as true sexually as it is socially. Aquarians are on earth to shake things up. Life is not safe and Aquarius knows this. Remember it the next time you have your Aquarius in bed!

Element: Air
Planet: Uranus
Best Trait: Friend to all
Worst Trait: Sometimes vapid or shallow

Pisces (February 19–March 20)

Pisceans use their personal and moral weakness to manipulate others. It often takes years before those involved in a relationship with a Pisces can come to grips and realize this. Often the partners of a Pisces are so distracted by the Piscean's problems that it takes a while before they recognize the ever present "crisis and rescue" cycles in the love affair or romance. Pisceans frequently spend their entire lives trying to discover some overall pattern, some destiny or a power that will enable them to sort out their lives and make sense of it all.

Thus, Pisceans become addicted to the idea of finding a rescuer, a nurse, a knight on a white charger, or just a regular mate who will wave a magic wand and set their lives straight. Pisces' life is a damned mess and it's your damned fault! Why didn't you fix them up like they asked you to?

Sending out alarms, such as going on binges, suicidal gestures, and even bizarre religious conversions are ways Pisces learns to manipulate. Perhaps it is unconscious, as most of Pisces' impulses are; however, it's important to recognize that this can poison the relationships of even the most compatible of partners. The greatest thing you can do for Pisces (who, like a little newborn fawn, can't stand on his own wobbly legs) is leave him alone to figure it out. Once Pisces gets up, allow him to stand without interfering. Pisces sometimes needs to understand that the best hand he can hold onto is his own.

Element: Water
Planet: Neptune
Best Trait: An innate, unassuming saintliness
Worst Trait: Playing the victim because it's easier

THE ELEMENTS OF LOVE

ARIES—Fire
TAURUS—Earth
GEMINI—Air
CANCER—Water
LEO—Fire
VIRGO—Earth
LIBRA—Air
SCORPIO—Water
SAGITTARIUS—Fire
CAPRICORN—Earth
AQUARIUS—Air
PISCES—Water

The physical nature of the universe is divided into the four elements found in astrology: Fire, Earth, Air, and Water. These four elements symbolize the fundamental nature of humankind and the plant and animal worlds. After all, anything that has a beginning has a horoscope. Love is one area where the four elements in astrology are particularly important. In our horoscopes, the elements represent our essential natures. Your Sun sign is one element found in your horoscope, but there are others. The Moon sign is yet another element and the element of your Rising sign is of great importance as well. This is taken throughout the remaining planets, but the Sun, Moon, and Rising signs are usually the most important.

Your Sun, Moon, and Rising signs may all be the same element, or they may all be different elements. Two or more signs of the same element indicate that this element is particularly strong in your chart. (For instance, maybe your Sun sign is Fire, while your Moon and Rising signs are Earth. Combine these two elements in your reading.)

In romance, the four elements must achieve balance in the combined horoscopes of you and your lover. If one natal chart is laden with planets and the Ascendant in Water signs, and your lover's chart has none, this could potentially create difficulties, yet if both charts include Earth signs, this is considered to be generally good since Water and Earth are harmonious. Of course, there may be other traits that bode well for the success of the relationship since the natal horoscope is very complex, with hundreds, if not thousands, of other factors. One good way to discover compatibility between you and your lover is to consider the elements in your individual charts. This can also be "generally" known just by looking at your Sun signs. The following are brief descriptions of the traits and compatibility of the four elements.

FIRE (ARIES–LEO–SAGITTARIUS)

Fire signs represent spirited attractions. Fire signs generally "play the field" and go where the action is. There is always a sense of urgency to every new relationship. After all, Fire signs are known for their passions and also their nobility. Left to their own devices,

Fire signs marry or commit a little later than the other elements. They are freedom-loving and spontaneous. To Fire signs, commitment threatens an end to their freedom. Naturally, Fire signs want to avoid marriage and settling down as long as possible. Fire signs spend their lives in love with freedom of thought and action. Metaphysically speaking, Fire signs stand for the burning fires of the human spirit. A chart strong in Fire signs will feature individuality and the ability to conquer lower forces.

Most Compatible Element: Other Fire signs
The Next Most Compatible Element: Air signs
The Least Compatible Element: Water signs

EARTH (TAURUS–VIRGO–CAPRICORN)

As the most dense element of all, the element of Earth stands for matter or the physical form. In this way, the astrological signs represented by the element of Earth are most interested in practical matters, the here and now, and most things that you can see and touch. Earth signs seldom lose their common sense when involved in love affairs. Practical matters and plans for the future include career, social standing, and finances. You'd be hard-pressed to find an Earth sign who completely loses his head in love. They are generally cautious when entering relationships, taking a "wait and see" attitude. Earth signs often choose persons with whom they feel the most comfortable, rather than on looks or personality alone. This rarely means a partner who is exciting or daring. Earth signs go for the familiar and what feels "safe." Earth signs also do best with lovers who are calm, and sometimes end up with lovers or spouses who are "brotherly-sisterly" or "fatherly-motherly." Earth signs look for stability and peace in warmly lit houses with white picket fences. They tend to dislike changes, especially shocks and surprises when it comes to dating, romance, and sex. Earth signs play it safe. Return their love and they will stay your most ardent protectors.

Most Compatible Element: Other Earth signs
The Next Most Compatible Element: Water signs
The Least Compatible Element: Air signs

AIR (GEMINI–LIBRA–AQUARIUS)

Air signs fly with ideas. To them, thought means everything. Their passion is for the mind, rather than the heart or even sex. Therefore, being in love with an Air sign (when you aren't one of them) can be puzzling. They have this strange detachment from their own emotions, as if they can stand far away and watch as strangers viewing themselves. The most emotional Air signs seem to get is when they are nervous. At other times, they may seem aloof or cold, but don't get them wrong. Air signs are as capable of passion and emotion as anyone else. It's just they are objective about themselves, not to mention that they dissect and analyze their feelings and impulses. Yes, as hard as it is to believe, Air signs really are mere mortals. Those born under the element of Air are quite interested in the concept of the soulmate because, after all, Air signs are looking for equal partners in love, rather than lovers who fulfill the roles of worshipers, children, or slaves. Air signs are fabulous, tireless, if not nervous, lovers, as long as they become infatuated with either your mind or something that you know. Air signs can inspire others through their flights of fancy. They are humane, intellectual, and alert. They believe in a higher purpose for all humankind.

Most Compatible Element: Other Air signs
The Next Compatible Element: Fire signs
The Least Compatible Element: Earth signs

WATER (CANCER–SCORPIO–PISCES)

Water signs are the most romantic lovers of all. Their greatest powers are the stirring effects of their imaginations and feelings of compassion for everyone. Water signs tend to understand their lovers on a core level. Often, when in a relationship with a Water sign, you will feel as if you have never been so understood by a lover. This doesn't mean that romances with Water signs are necessarily better. It just means that Water signs have an innate capacity to know and understand how you feel. That is, of course, unless you fall out of favor with your particular Water sign. Feelings get submerged and it doesn't take long for the water to turn to ice. If, however, you are looking for empathy and being understood, Water signs are the ones to turn to for romance and love. The inner world of feeling and the imagination is pronounced in all of the Water signs. Of course, the ability to empathize varies, with Pisces showing the greatest potential for empathy and Scorpio showing the least. Yet the ability of all three Water signs to feel and connect is unusually strong if not overdrawn. Water signs tend to get swept away by their passions and for this reason they typically do not enter into romances and relationships too easily. They realize what toil or sacrifice romance can bring about and they also wonder if they can survive it. This often makes them very reluctant lovers. It is hard to earn the trust of a Water sign, but once this is accomplished, they are completely yours. Learn to surrender to the powers of love. Your Water sign will surely show you how this is done!

Most Compatible Element: Other Water signs
The Next Most Compatible Element: Earth signs
The Least Compatible Element: Fire signs

Please keep in mind that natal horoscopes are often made up of the four different elements, usually emphasizing one or two elements, rather than all four. Therefore, if you are a Water sign, you may also have Fire signs in your chart. This would enhance your compatibility with a Fire sign lover. The same would be true of the other signs and elements as well. In comparing horoscopes, it's always nice to have a computer printout of your natal chart, as well as the chart of your lover. These are available for free on many Web sites over the Internet, or can be purchased for a few dollars if ordered through the mail. You can find addresses of places that sell birth charts in many popular astrology magazines or astrology calendars.

Although compatibility between the four elements in your chart and your lover's is important in keeping the love affair alive, the place to begin a relationship is through the fine art of attraction and seduction. Do you know what it takes to draw to yourself what you need in a lover? Are you aware of the ideal way to seduce the lover of your dreams? Read on and learn the astrological art of seduction by looking at the twelve signs and beyond!

TWO

SEDUCTION
AND THE TWELVE
ASTROLOGICAL SIGNS:
WHAT DO THEY REALLY
WANT?

The individual styles of the twelve astrological signs determine how we relate to others. Naturally, this includes romance, sex, and the art of seduction. One of the biggest mistakes we make in our relationships, and this includes relationships of all kinds, is that we assume others are just like ourselves. Of course, this is a highly democratic idea and, at its best, has some degree of truth, but not always when it comes to our choices in love and styles of relating.

When it is not true, and often it is not, we end up with bitter misunderstandings because we assume that our lovers, and others, have the exact same values, tastes, preferences, and even morals that we do. Obviously, this is not the case. This is especially not the case once you begin to understand the ancient wisdom and science of astrology. Other people are like us, but they are also different.

We see this no more clearly than in our closest relationships. This is why so many marriages and relationships end. We think our partners should do just as we do. Isn't that what we're all taught to believe?

Astrologers have always known of the distinct differences in people. There is no such thing as everyone being the same. We have various styles of relating. Of course, there are moments when we are close and similar to our lovers, but this is not always the case. So, what do we do when our lovers contradict our values? We become incensed. We think to ourselves, "Now why don't you do it the right way—which is my way?" or "Why do you want to be with people when I am feeling alone? Why do you like rain when I prefer sun?"

In romance and sex it is possible to avoid conflict. Once you understand what your lover expects or desires from the relationship, there will be far fewer clashes. One of the main areas of disagreement is in the area of sex. If not confronted and resolved, this can be a serious problem. The ways we seduce and are seduced are critical factors in determining our compatibility as life partners. Read on and learn what it is your lover wants and also what you like best.

ARIES

Aries is a gutsy Fire sign who usually comes on strong or in an overbearing way when sexually attracted. Naturally, this causes clashes of every imaginable kind in relationships. This is why romance remains an area of difficulty to Aries. The sign of the Ram, though friendly enough, does not flow well with others. Aries is simply too much of an individual and will fight for truth, territory, or whatever. This just means Aries aims to win. He forgets that such an attitude is inappropriate in romance. He also forgets that not all people are blood-and-guts types like he is. Aries views everyone as "friend or foe." You are either with him or against him. One can just imagine how this gets in the way of sex and romance. Aries doesn't want his lovers to have a different opinion or view because it threatens his. With patience, this sign can grow into a passionate lover few can top—as long as you are willing to allow Aries to *stay* on top!

The Way Aries Seduces: Aries appears bristling and confrontational at first. This is one way you can be sure Aries is attracted. He seems angry because he fears that once he is sexually smitten, he will lose his power. You can expect Aries to back away for a while and then come on very forcefully, not taking "no" for an answer. Aries fears that your sexual power will cause him to lose his. Power is not something Aries wants to lose at any cost, especially when it comes to affairs of the heart. Therefore, when Aries is seducing you, he may act odd or moody. The more he is smitten, the more he will disappear for a while. Let Aries have his space, but hold your ground. In the beginning, never show Aries any weakness on your part. Aries seduces with his passions, which are grand. Show Aries that yours are just as grand.

The Way Aries Is Seduced: Aries is seduced by the one thing that everyone else wants. *Be that.* The sign of the Ram goes for the most desirable person in the room. It brings out his natural urge to compete and win the grand prize—that prize is *you*, of course. Make sure you measure up to these standards if you become interested in an Aries. Act with the confidence that you are "God's gift" at that moment. (Aries certainly will have no problem with that.) Act only a little interested in Aries; appear to be interested in others as well. There is nothing like competition to get Aries all stirred up. Also, brush Aries off every now and then. Don't be as mean as he is capable of being; Aries is actually quite sensitive, so watch it. When you two become closer, massage his tired temples, then pull on his ears. Kiss him deeply while doing so. This drives Aries out of his head.

TAURUS

You'll feel relaxed around Taurus, a stubborn yet calm sign. Taurus has charisma, but you may not notice it right away. The sign of the bull is both steadfast and laid back. Taurus is strong, but *rarely comes on strong*. He is a patient lover and a sign that you grow to love over time, making you wonder why you didn't get carried away with the love affair even sooner. You can be sure Taurus is understated, but this sign usually attracts what he needs by going about things at his own pace. Naturally, this includes romance and sex. Don't expect quick developments in that department. You shouldn't force the issue. Taurus hates being rushed. This tower of power and sensuality instinctively knows when to make his move. So trust this most trustworthy sign.

The Way Taurus Seduces: How? Slow and easy! Taurus usually seduces with money and gifts. Don't be insulted. Taurus isn't trying to buy your love. This is what he was taught as a child. When you love someone, you should shower him or her with *things*— usually beautiful or precious objects, gifts that show you really care. Taurus values money and material possessions greatly. He assumes that you do, too. Taurus also seduces by being supple, soft, and always affectionate whereby he becomes a "safe area" or "comfort zone." After all, what seems to be an affectionate teddy bear is really a gentle bull. Bask in the luxury of this sign's attention and love.

The Way Taurus Is Seduced: Being full-figured doesn't hurt when trying to attract a Taurus Bull—unless your Taurus is one of those odd types who prefer lovers to be skinny and, believe me, this is rare. He goes for curvaceous legs, too, so show your gams a lot. Having curly hair and dimples attracts Taureans of either sex. Taurus women look for a full, brawny chest in their men. Taurus is also seduced in the same way he initially seduces you— that is, by a show of money and gifts. Taurus is practical, so attracting his attention by showing you are successful in different areas of your life will keep this sign's attention. Also, kisses on the nape of the neck work wonders in turning a Taurus on!

GEMINI

Small talk and a lot of eye contact are the devices that Gemini uses in order to attract. Gemini is a friendly Air sign, thus he uses curiosity and charm to make his first moves—so much so, that it is often difficult to sort out whether Gemini wants you to be his lover or his friend. This is because he wants you to be both. To Gemini, love can't exist without friendship and intriguing conversation. After all, Gemini is more of a mental sign than a romantic sign. Keep this in mind when it seems as if Gemini is more interested in the way you think and perceive than in how you perform in bed. Don't get me wrong. Gemini is just as sexual as any other sign, but he appreciates the mind first. Other good things, such as intimacy and sex, will quickly follow the first friendly words.

The Way Gemini Seduces: You'll notice that Gemini appears to be absolutely *fascinated* by you! He usually starts off with outrageous flirting, winking, staring, and touching you. Gemini is the most flirtatious sign of all. If Gemini doesn't flirt, then he must be dead. After some serious flirting, Gemini will use his wit to make you laugh. He'll bring up the news of the day, all the while finding out more about you. Stick around Gemini for a few minutes, and you will realize that Gemini is the most dynamic conversationalist and the best kisser you have ever met.

The Way Gemini Is Seduced: You can seduce vivacious Gemini, a sign that is intellectually insatiable, by using your mind. Although Gemini likes to see a lot of thigh and leg, it is the power of your mind and intellect that initially attracts. Also, try anything unusual. He won't care, as long as there is humor and imagination behind it all. Allow Gemini to call you often, but don't call him. Ask Gemini lots of questions and listen patiently to the answers. This will put Gemini at ease. Kiss, hold hands, stand close, and rub shoulders. Whisper something that Gemini doesn't already know in his ear. Gemini is forever impressed by people who know more than he does.

CANCER

This cautious Water sign is highly romantic, but Cancers remain shy or secretive over the whole issue of love and sex. Cancer is an inordinately cautious sign, and it may take a while to figure out if a Cancer is truly interested or not. Cancer people are impossible to read, as they hold most of their emotions bottled up inside. There are ways, however, that show Cancers are attracted. First of all, Cancers will tend to use a very gentle manner of speech with you if they're romantically smitten. Cancers will also have trouble maintaining eye contact, and their gaze will often sweep the ground somewhere around your feet. Cancers find it very difficult to be direct with people. If you give a Cancer love and extra space, then watch your Cancer blossom. Cancer, though thoroughly sensitive, is in essence a strong sign. Shower this Water sign with your love.

The Way Cancer Seduces: Cancer seduces by remaining coy and somewhat in the background at first. Cancer will seem very remote, and he is too shy to flirt with you. What you see is the gentle smile and downcast eyes. Keep in mind: Cancer is sizing you up for future romantic action. A Cancer will first watch you from afar. This sign does not make quick moves. It takes Cancer a while to work up his courage. Cancer wants to make sure *it feels right* before plunging into a love affair. Usually, Cancer has been hurt and doesn't want to make the same mistake twice. After you have gained Cancer's trust, and the wall has been broken through, you may be surprised at how passionate and attentive to your needs Cancer can be.

The Way Cancer Is Seduced: Obviously, Cancer loves the chest. Doing something that draws attention to the chest is one good way to seduce a Cancer initially; however, be discreet. Cancer is not a sign that normally goes for anything that smacks of sleaze. An open blouse revealing a bit of cleavage or some ruffles or an elegant collar framing the breasts, are attention-grabbers for the Cancer you have in mind. Those born under the influence of the Moon are sensual but not particularly lustful. Cancer is more interested in being understood and having an emotional connection with someone than in having an empty love affair with someone with a certain body type or with a lover who is "built," as they used to say. For this reason, those born under the sign of Cancer are seduced by a person with reasonable attractiveness who is most tuned into their needs.

LEO

This is a sign that is born to shine. Leo loves the spotlight and, at first, won't mind sharing a stage with you. In fact, many of Leo's lovers are trophy pieces whom he loves to show off to his friends. Yes, this can seem empty when you're looking for something a little more meaningful and serious. There are ways to win this sign's heart and respect. Look and act more important than he does. Be a person worthy of admiration. I know it's hard to top a Leo. Like Aries, he can't stand other people being "on top." Yet in many ways, he admires a lover who can beat him at his own game. Leos are attracted to people who are minor or major celebrities at what they do. They'll grab whatever attention they can, even when it's based on the talent and influence of other lovers and friends. The sign of the Lion prefers cutting-edge people who are always involved in interesting or risk-taking activities. Look to Leo for inspiration and be the kind of person that he or she admires.

The Way Leo Seduces: The primary way Leo seduces is by being the most attractive and interesting person in the room. For Leo, everything is pomp and circumstance. So, it is not surprising that this is also how Leo approaches romance and sex. Leo will come on to you like a star, and with the attitude that you should be flattered by the attention. Those not initially impressed by Leo's chewing on the scenery may eventually come to believe that Leo really is the greatest one in the room, and how dare you turn this enormous prize down? Leo appears poised and confident. It is an *affectation*, of course. Leos are insecure like everyone else. Leo wears his heart on his sleeve. You'll not find a more passionate lover anywhere.

The Way Leo Is Seduced: Very simple—individuals born under the sign of Leo are seduced primarily by attention and flattery. In fact, Leo is one of the easier signs to manipulate. It doesn't get too complex: just act as if you think Leo is the greatest—but within certain limits. Leo will appreciate that you need to be the center of attention, too. And there are many ways to do this. When you go out with Leo, change your hair or wear something quite different from your normal style. Talk about a timely subject that most people in your circle, including Leo, don't know very much about. Don't drone on; just be fascinated in and dramatic about your subject matter. Act as if you are just as worthy of attention as Leo is. The need to feel admired is something Leo understands. During times of closeness or intimacy, place Leo's hand on your chest so he can feel your beating heart. Leo will find this wildly mesmerizing.

VIRGO

Expect some shyness and hesitancy from Virgo. This is one sign that often feels awkward in the areas of seduction and romance. Virgo fears he'll mess up badly and be subject to ridicule or criticism. Those born under the sign of Virgo wish desperately to please, but they are always convinced that they won't. In Virgo's eyes, everyone else seems greater and so much more deserving. Deep-seated insecurity is something that plagues Virgo for a lifetime, even when he is at the pinnacle of success. Reassuring Virgo throughout the relationship is the best way to keep the fires of romance stoked. Let Virgo know how much he pleases you, both in and out of the bedroom. Don't dwell on criticism, whether it is coming from you or your Virgo. Too much criticism can destroy or alter any future happiness with your Virgo love, so tread softly on Virgo's tender heart.

The Way Virgo Seduces: With difficulty, because this sign surely lacks nerve. Virgo, however, is the sign of the helper; thus, he will often strike up a relationship by doing favors and all kinds of little "extras" so you'll know for sure that he likes you. Virgo feels most at ease in the role of the servant, but not in a way that lacks nobility. When Virgo is in love or is attracted, he shows his affection in tangible ways—not in faint whispers and empty promises of passion, but with real substance. Sometimes Virgo plays the loner and seduces by his moodiness and vulnerability. Virgo can be very charismatic when left to his own devices. As soon as you gain his trust, the shyness goes away and you find yourself with a lover who is humorous, sensual, and humane. He also does really nice things with his hands.

The Way Virgo Is Seduced: Consider becoming close friends with him first. Never sleep with a Virgo too quickly. I have in mind as an example one relationship between a Sagittarius and a Virgo. The romance lasted for two years, but when it ended, Virgo bitterly remarked, "Why did you sleep with me on our first date? I suppose you do that with all the guys?" In other words, the romance was doomed from the start. Yet Virgo is not as puritanical as most books claim. In fact, Virgos can be kind of ballsy. Nevertheless, he is certainly pious in many ways and tends toward having old-fashioned mores. One seduces a Virgo by reassurances. Pet and play. With Virgo, you will want to *coax* intimacy and use gentle words and gentle touch.

LIBRA

This social, outgoing sign is easy to get to know. Venus-ruled Libra has no trouble collecting lovers. Everyone is a little bit in love with Libra anyway. Because Librans like to go "out and about" while circulating among friends and strangers alike, they are not as assertive so much as they are simply popular. If you want someone to deliver disappointing news for you, just call Libra. Not only are Librans typically the most beautiful sign, they are the smoothest in making everyone feel better. For Libra, every relationship means "connections." Always needing to be with someone,

Libra gets romantically involved quite often. All you have to do to attract Libra is to smile, look good, and act interested in what Libra has to say. Keep in mind, however, that Libra is easily attracted, and you may be one of many.

The Way Libra Seduces: Charmers from the crib to the grave, Librans know how to make someone feel desired. This is one of the reasons they stay so popular. Libra also seduces with oozing sensuality, with delicious sights and smells, with an ability to put others at ease, and by gorgeous bedroom eyes. Good looks, which Libra has plenty of, doesn't hurt either. Libra is quite impeccable when it comes to dress and grooming. Typical Librans are a feast for the nose and eyes. To Librans everything is both casual and beautiful. Librans smile, blush, sip their drinks, and hang on your every word. When around a Libra, you simply feel more loved than usual. No matter that the passion doesn't run very deep, it feels damn good at the time.

The Way Libra Is Seduced: To Libra, you should first appear to be a *beautiful object*, a much-desired, delectable prize. Although this may seem shallow in the beginning, Libra is very sensitive to how things look. Librans can't stand ugliness. That's no problem, however; in this day and age, you can always dress up ugliness. Yet if you don't at least look *interesting* and you aren't attired in the finest threads, it is highly possible Libra will overlook your other attributes, no matter how fine. Keep in mind, you don't have to be drop-dead gorgeous—but your clothes and perfume should be. You don't have to be rich—just look as if you are. After the initial attraction is cemented, make sure you've read up on the latest book or movie. Libra is impressed and seduced by good taste and is often disappointed in mere mortals.

♏

SCORPIO

Despite Scorpio's reputation for lust, he is really rather backward when it comes to initiating romance and sex. After all, Scorpios are like any other Water sign. They stick their toe in the water before making the plunge. Scorpio is hesitant and basically not very trusting when it comes to affairs of the heart. Scorpio is also known to be possessive and sometimes jealous, so you would do well not to dwell on past relationships or ever mention sex with other people. Although Scorpio may go in for odd sex once in a while, you can be sure that this type of sex is not with someone he cares about. Speaking of your sexual indiscretions—just *don't*. Never talk to a Scorpio about having sex with anyone other than him. If you do, watch Scorpio ice over. Scorpio may forgive, once or twice, but this stinging bug does not forget. Yes, there will be passion, but it is controlled. All in all, Scorpios are stable, but most of the time they take it to the extreme.

The Way Scorpio Seduces: It's easy to sense when a Scorpio is interested. Scorpio is like a cat focusing on his prey. Scorpio seduces with his intensity and his gaze. He doesn't give up, either. Once he has you in mind, you will undoubtedly bend under his will. Almost everyone does. That's how powerful a Scorpio's desire is. To a Scorpio, desire is everything; passion and intention run a close second and third. We all know what those dime-store astrology books say about Scorpio. Think of Bela Lugosi as *Dracula* and his attraction to women. It was in his eyes—for Charles Manson, too, another Scorpio. Before I weird you out, though, I must say that Scorpio is a rather gentle sign and very loving. All in all, Scorpio is here to make his mark with that stinger of his. Sex is one way to do this. It goes without saying that you haven't been loved until you've been loved by a Scorpio.

The Way Scorpio Is Seduced: It's interesting to note that this most complex of astrological signs is really not that complex when it comes to sexual attraction. Scorpio is best seduced by overt sexual suggestion, like boobs falling out of the dress or clothes that are tight or very sheer. The world of sex is the world of fantasy to a Scorpio. It is as well to the other signs, except Scorpio tends to be a bit more focused on it than the other signs. It's not that sex means more. Nor does it mean that Scorpio is necessarily more highly sexed. It simply means that Scorpio has a highly sexual imagination. It takes very little to kindle this desire. Just peruse a sexy catalogue; you'll get the right picture.

SAGITTARIUS

To attract a Sagittarius, give the impression that you're having more fun than a barrel of monkeys! In fact, step out on that dance floor and dance like an ape! Sagittarians love wildness. They are optimistic and they like people who are the same. Even a light-hearted, silly attitude challenges the Sag to join your party. In essence, Sagittarius prefers friends and lovers who are free, open, and not afraid to laugh out loud. When Sagittarius goes to the outer limits of fun and pleasure, he wants to take others with him. Speaking of parties, Sagittarius is the sign that makes partying an art. In fact, expect your romance to start and carry on for a while in a group setting. This sign looks for people who can cheer him on and generally picks hooligans for friends. If you want a rousing good time with lots of laughs and incredible sex, find yourself a Sagittarius.

The Way Sagittarius Is Seduced: The sign of the Archer searches for adventure in all areas of his life. A daring romance where you and he break all kinds of rules will really turn a die-hard Sagittarius on. He's a rebel and he wants you to be, too. Rough-necking and talking a bit dirty will keep Sagittarius hanging about. Holding your own against a Sagittarius will sexually excite him. Don't be put off by the insults—it's his way of teasing. This is just one way to flirt. If you want to seduce a Sagittarius, wear denim with black leather. Wear jewelry with black leather and studs, the kind that would look good on a Great Dane. Make plans that don't include your Sagittarius and never sit by the phone waiting for his call. This will eat at him and make him wonder why he's not the greatest act in town. Treat Sagittarius as if he is *not* the most important thing in your life. Sagittarius wishes to be humbled, so humble him.

The Way Sagittarius Seduces: The teasing and playful insults that Sagittarius uses to get your attention are not meant to harm; they are his version of flirting. Perhaps not the best strategy, it is still meant to impress. Sagittarians love to debate and banter about. They're brutally truthful and think everyone else is the same way. Sagittarius comes on tough and taking on this lover is a big adventure that involves roughing it, the great outdoors, and staying close to the land. Basically, seduction is not the proper word when describing a Sagittarian's sexual intentions.

Sometimes Sagittarius takes you to one of his hideaways with lots of "atmosphere," like wobbly tables with candles stuck in beer bottles. At other times, Sagittarius just blurts out what he's after. If you're sensitive to bluntness or the truth, or you're sensitive to Sagittarius' version of the truth, you may want to reconsider. Sagittarius isn't too soft on softies.

CAPRICORN

It takes Capricorn a few tries before working up the nerve to approach a potential love mate. Capricorns are seldom at ease with romance, and for a while they tend to take out people they aren't serious about. They don't want to make a wrong decision and live to regret it. Most of their sex partners tend to be "flings." After all, Capricorn understands what a serious business romance is. Yet Capricorn lacks spontaneity and that can be a problem when starting a new romantic affair. It's hard to determine whether Capricorn is truly interested in anything more than sex or dating. Generally, if Capricorn is interested, he'll keep calling back. Expect some time to pass, as Capricorn will mull things over before committing. If you're worth it, though, they usually do. Like an oak tree, you can lean on Capricorn. Also like the oak tree, many Capricorns live to be about 100. Make sure you're in it for the long run!

The Way Capricorn Is Seduced: You can inflame the romantic interest of a Capricorn by dropping the names of all of the important people that you know. Like Scorpios, Capricorns confuse power with sex. They believe that the more powerful and influential they appear, the more easily they can seduce you. Capricorn tries to impress people with his possessions and connections. He really doesn't love things that much; he just feels a little empty inside. Capricorn has spent so many years denying his emotional needs that he completely loses touch with them. It takes a while to stimulate the very things he has buried over: his inner life and his feelings. If you really want to snag Capricorn, become aware of the needs of his body. Capricorn rules the skeletal frame. A full body massage can do wonders for the relationship. Show Capricorn how good you are with your hands.

The Way Capricorn Seduces: When a Capricorn seduces, you can expect a lot of big talk about his "connections" and what he can do for you. This is not bad, as Capricorn tends to think in a practical way even when it comes to sex and romance. For Capricorn, there must always be some "pay-off," though. Expect to hear many promises of wealth, power, and influence. You see, Capricorn—like his opposite sign, Cancer—feels so insecure. Capricorn individuals believe they don't deserve love, affection, or sex unless they can impress you in some other way. Their way is usually in the areas of financial worth and social importance. Capricorn has many ambitious dreams, and he is often a very tender lover. Talking about great plans can only bring you closer. Join Capricorn in his talk of pipe dreams and big plans. In this way, the seduction part of your relationship will be mutual.

AQUARIUS

They often call themselves "eccentric" and take pride in being stranger than just about anyone else on the planet, and I'm not about to contradict this. In romance, the Aquarian is looking for a lover who is as rare and unique as he is, but also a lover who has many interesting things to show and teach him. For Aquarius, the most fascinating and stimulating things that happen are in his own mind. This includes sex. Aquarius prefers sex in a game setting or on a TV screen. Aquarians are not personal, they are mental to the max. Therefore, all physical attractions will take a backseat to whatever kind of intelligence the potential lover might have. Those born under the sign of Aquarius can tolerate silliness and the inane, but they can't stand ignorance or bigotry—unless, of course, it's their own brand of bigotry, meaning they don't tolerate stupid people very well. The Aquarian stands for brotherhood and sister-hood, but he nevertheless disdains anything *common*. He is simply in favor of uniqueness, uncommon lovers, and famous friends. Yet don't forget—Aquarius is most in favor of himself.

The Way Aquarius Is Seduced: Dress and act like a lunatic. Be very assured in your ability to produce moments of weirdness and far-out experiences. Talk about the future. Confess that you're married to your computer and you don't need a woman or man. Cut your hair very short and dye it green. Ring your eyes with silver. Mention you know a few vampires—*real ones*. Say that you can talk to aliens, too. Dress in a way that is more typi-cal of the opposite sex. If you're a man, wear plaid knee socks and a kilt. If you're a woman, smoke a cigar and wear a tie. Nothing turns an Aquarius on as much as the *suggestion* of gender-bending. Some Aquarians are more conservative than others and won't admit to anything that seems too kinky. The real truth is, we all love this sexual cross-reference to a certain degree—such as beautiful women in men's suits and men with gorgeous hair. Perhaps it's because there is a bit of Aquarius in us all.

The Way Aquarius Seduces: Most typically, Aquarians first approach you as friends, with a great deal of curiosity about you and your *experiences*. Expect lots of questions. As friendship grows, love will deepen. Aquarius will then show you secret sides of himself and his interests, which are *very* important. Aquarius will come to know your mind and your deepest yearnings even more than you understand them yourself. Aquarius is a very sweet lover, very forgiving of flaws. After all, Aquarius finds your *flaws* interesting. Aquarius will seduce you by completely accepting you, unconditionally and without judgment. He will insist that his friends love you as well. This unique personality has the ability to make everyone feel special. It is a sign that fascinates and enthralls.

PISCES

Pisceans are drawn to lovers that they *perceive* to be strong and to have a direction, but this sign is easily fooled. Pisces' perceptions of others are nebulous, to say the least. This is quite odd because Pisceans are also psychic—that is, unless it has to do with themselves. Throughout their lives, Pisceans are famous for making the wrong decisions, or making the *right* decision at the *wrong* time, often realizing too late who actually loves them the most. Many of their romances turn out to be mishaps and lapses in judgment. There is hope, however; Pisces functions well in relationships with people who have both common sense and imagination. The trick is to find a lover who has noble intentions, meaning one who refuses to lie to Pisces. Pisceans are drawn to fantasy even more than romance. Mean or controlling people can destroy the spirit of a Pisces, but lax or deceitful lovers kill Pisces in mind, body, and soul. A stable individual with a kind heart, a lover who isn't afraid to take the lead, is the best possible partner for a Pisces.

The Way Pisces Seduces: Pisces is a sign of contradictions. After all, Pisceans contain the elements of all twelve signs. Everything about them is true. Everything about them is false. They are very good. They are very bad. Pisces has been portrayed in popular astrology as the angelic Mermaid; her father of the seas, noble Neptune; and Jesus on the Cross, or God of all waters. This is why it seems a contradiction to say that Pisces often seduces by acting or dressing in a provocative or titillating manner. Pisces understands the power of the image—as a seedy pornographic image is used to attract lovers, and as a siren uses her voice to attract the souls of ship-wrecked sailors. Pisces is often the most glamorous and seductive of all of the astrological signs. Pisceans plumb the depths of the soul, sex, and the emotions. This Mermaid is also the most alluring. Like sea-salt, she gets into your blood!

The Way Pisces Is Seduced: Pisceans are soft and gentle, so there are many ingenious ways to seduce a Pisces. In fact, since Pisces can probably already read your mind, it won't even be very hard to lure her or him into the sack. To begin with, write Pisces a poem. Set the poem to music if you can. Pisces appreciates anything that comes from the heart and things born of the imagination; it doesn't necessarily have to be great. You can also seduce Pisces by creating an evocative and mysterious atmosphere with flickering candlelight, wafting perfumes, satin sheets, small tokens wrapped up in curious boxes, conversation near a waterfall or fountain—things that suggest color and mood, like ocean and starlight. Be imaginative. Be kind to Pisces and he will be yours.

As you know, there are certain signs, such as Aries or Scorpio, who need very little encouragement when it comes to the art of seduction and romance. These signs already know how to make the right move that leads to intimacy and sex. Other zodiac signs, such as Cancer or Virgo, are more retiring and may need a nudge or lots of encouragement when it comes to the complex and often intimidating areas of love and romance. Coming on to your lover in the most appropriate way possible can only lead to romantic success. This will in turn lead to the greatest pleasure in our mortal lives: intimacy and sex.

THREE

VENUS AND MARS—LOVE IN THE STARS

Venus and Mars frolic and play together as lovers do on a Grecian urn. It's no wonder. These planets are never far away from each other. In fact, they are two sides of the same mirror—but one radiates the power of the male essence while the other governs the mysteries of female sexuality. They are opposite yet joined, like faces on a coin.

When we look at our universe astrologically through a map of the skies, Venus and Mars are never more than one sign away from each other. Ancient astrologers attributed male and female characteristics to these planets. We now know, however, that the specific energies of Venus and Mars exist in men and women alike. We each have feminine and masculine components in our natures. We also know that in order to have a stable love relationship or a sexually satisfying romance, these planets of love and sex must complement each other in positive ways. An ill-fated romance is generally one that lacks harmonious aspects between Venus and Mars. (These harmonious Venus and Mars aspects appear not only in the charts of lovers; they are often found in the charts of close friends.)

Although the ancients, as well as modern astrologers, see Venus and Mars governing romance, these planets have other meanings. They are, in fact, called "inner planets," meaning that they deal with personal and lesser issues more than with universal problems, such as power and war. These planets are not about skirting or dodging the obvious. They are not about one-night stands or high school crushes. They are not even really about marriage.

Venus and Mars have much more to do with sexual magnetism. They rule physical attraction, satisfying sex, and erotic play. Yes, this kind of sexual compatibility can lead to more serious areas such as marriage, but it doesn't have to. In some instances, a powerful magnetism between Venus and Mars can mean that sex is the only thing the partners have in common. Yet the romantic relationships that work out best are those in which Venus and Mars complement each other.

For the relationship to progress to more serious matters, such as commitment and marriage, these love planets must make strong and flowing aspects to each other. Read on and see if your Venus or Mars matches those of your lover. If not, at least you can learn what your lover truly desires.

HER VENUS

VENUS IN ARIES

A woman with her Venus in Aries is searching for a "real man," the kind she can play with and compete against. Her love life must have a marked physical component. Only the strong can rise to her standards. In general, a sensitive man is not what she wants, although she may claim to differ. The Venus-in-Aries woman wants to dominate the one she loves, but the minute her partner becomes submissive, she will lose respect for him. Romance to her is like a hunt. She is searching for someone who is stronger than she is, but do not dare try to break her spirit.

Sexually, this woman enjoys intense lovemaking sessions. She prefers sexual intercourse to be rough and fast. For her, sex is like a workout that relieves tension. Strangely, the Venus-in-Aries woman longs for the guy who treats her the worst. She mistakes compassion and caring for weakness. While Venus in Aries prefers domination and control, she secretly wishes her love partner would take a stand. This woman is a vigorous lover, and her mate will enjoy an interesting sex life.

It's important, however, to remember to show your strength with a Venus-in-Aries woman. If not, she might abuse you in a verbal way or opt to go with someone else. Learn to appreciate this woman's need for adventure and challenge. Remain strong and also brash. (Venus in Aries finds intimidation sexually arousing.) Understand that when Venus in Aries needs to fight, you should take your stand. Afterward, allow it to blow over. Things will run more smoothly if you do.

Most Compatible Mars Signs: Jaunty Mars in Sagittarius provides the kind of physical excitement that Venus in Aries needs. Both are frank and honest about what they need sexually. Mars in Leo is charismatic and compelling. Both signs have strong wills to test the limits, which only makes things more interesting in the bedroom.

Interesting Combos in Case You're Looking for Fireworks: Mars in Libra idolizes women and isn't intimidated by Amazons, such as

Venus in Aries. Although different in their approach (Venus in Aries can seem pushy while Mars in Libra appears soft and polite), these opposite signs naturally complement each other. Venus in Aries cannot go wrong with a Mars-in-Scorpio man—he can go on for hours.

Mars Signs to Avoid Like the Plague: Astrological signs that tend to be overly sensitive, such as Mars in Virgo, Mars in Cancer, or Mars in Pisces, do not get along well with combative Venus in Aries. She could potentially view all of these signs as weak individuals whom she could defeat in two seconds flat. Although these Mars signs would be attuned to what she needs, she would not be able to respect them.

VENUS IN TAURUS

Just call her "beauty," because she certainly is. Venus in Taurus is sensual from birth. This voluptuous charmer breathes and lives romance, but she is not obsessed by it. She is generally a laid-back type. She adores exploring the landscape of a gorgeous man, preferring those who are hairy, with long hair, and a strange sense of humor—a lover who is like a laughing pagan god. Jim Morrison would be her ideal type. Few talk about the fact that Taurus can be as sexual as Scorpio (the uninhibited ones, that is), but the truth of the matter is, Venus in Taurus has a powerful sexual appetite and is a regular horny toad. Sometimes she can't get enough. Her sex drive even surpasses her love for shopping and rich foods.

Venus in Taurus is a languid lover. She loves to be nuzzled in her ears and on her neck. Have you ever seen paintings of odalisques? Plump women with white, fleshy bodies surrounded by flowers, idolized by lovers, attended to by slaves, and reclining on a brocade couch? These old masterpiece paintings fit Venus in

Taurus to a T. Except, unlike Venus in Aries, Venus in Taurus is compassionate to her love-slaves. She is stubborn but not mean.

Venus in Taurus demands that she be pampered and taken care of. She expects all of the rewards that love and sex can bring her. She is an eager fan of the trappings of sexual love: dancing candles, an Auryvedic massage, and well-thumbed copies of the Kama Sutra. Sex to this touchy-feely woman is akin to a full, satisfying meal. Venus in Taurus takes a while to reach orgasm, but when she does, it is quite intense. Give her time. Meet her needs. This woman is a true virtuoso when it comes to the sexual flames of passion and attraction.

Most Compatible Mars Signs: Mars in Virgo and Mars in Capricorn are natural lovers for Venus in Taurus since they share her earthiness. They also make stable lovers, and this is important to the way Taurus responds sexually because she requires patient foreplay. Generally, these signs also make good partners for long-term relationships, but they are rarely as sexually hot as she is. In addition, Virgo and Capricorn men are chronic worriers, and this can sometimes dampen the natural optimism of a Taurus.

Interesting Combos in Case You're Looking for Fireworks: Hands down, Mars in Scorpio is the sign that sends Venus in Taurus to the moon and stars. Both signs love sex and place great value on a satisfying sexual life. In fact, Scorpio may be one of the few lovers who can take Taurus to the heights of passion and orgasm. Another interesting sexual partner for her is Mars in Leo. Both are fixed signs, and this creates an interesting sexual tension that is always present. These two signs tend to rub each other the wrong way—except in the case of sex—when they rub each other in all of the right ways possible!

Mars Signs to Avoid Like the Plague: Mars in Aquarius can be a bit kinky for the sometimes plain Jane Taurus. Taurus isn't into bizarre surprises (such as a lover confessing his bisexuality—no, she probably won't understand). Strangeness and variety are not traits Venus in Taurus is looking for in the bedroom. Instead, she desires constancy and passion—not a natural state for Mars in Aquarius. Mars in Gemini can seem fickle and childish to a Taurus, even though these side-by-side signs share some of the same planets. Mars in Gemini tends to prattle on, and Taurus is fond of warm skin, not cool emotions and empty words.

VENUS IN GEMINI

She has a boyish quality that is attractive to both sexes. This woman can be a gifted sexual acrobat or an androgynous fairy sprite. Even so, Venus in Gemini looks for versatility in lovers and isn't afraid to indulge in experimental positions, threesomes, or phone sex. It's not that she's promiscuous. She's just curious. She loves sex and can have many lovers, but she takes it all lightly. Venus in Gemini is not enslaved by the power of Eros.

For this whimsical Twin, sex is pretty much of a distraction anyway. She isn't into long, drawn-out lovemaking sessions. Conversely, she can reach an orgasm rather quickly, but then it's over with. Her orgasms are as intense as those of any other sign. It's just that Venus in Gemini isn't emotionally tied to sex. She'd rather lie around in her birthday suit and have a good chat.

If you want this woman for a lover, you will have to appreciate her mind and listen to her words. Words are gods to Gemini. When they say that the brain is the largest sexual organ in the body, this is especially true for Gemini. How you communicate with this woman verbally will make all the difference when it comes to lovemaking. What really attracts her are her lover's mind and wit.

Although Gemini seldom surrenders to the yoke of sexual power plays, she is a vivacious, imaginative lover. This sign makes love on purely nervous energy, and most of her lovers enjoy this. The climax of Venus in Gemini flutters on and on like the wings of a hummingbird. More than any other Venus sign, this sign is often capable of multiple orgasms. If you like peak experiences, sex with this woman soars. Lovemaking with Venus in Gemini is quick and ephemeral, like the blur of wings.

Most Compatible Mars Signs: Venus in Gemini flows best with the energy of Mars in Aquarius. Both are well educated when it comes to sex, whether or not they have much sexual experience. After all, when an Aquarius or a Gemini wants to learn a new technique, they both hit the books. Talking during sex is exciting to both, and the conversation that follows sex is often more interesting than the initial sex. These partners grow together very well sexually. Mars in Libra comes across as soft-spoken, gentle, and somewhat pretty. He has an androgynous look that greatly appeals to Gemini. Mars in Libra comes closest to being Venus in Gemini's knight in shining armor. For both signs, sex is definitely good— but the most important thing is the satisfaction of their eery telepathic connections and shared minds.

Interesting Combos in Case You're Looking for Fireworks: Mars in Sagittarius loves to explore and so does Venus in Gemini. Both go for excitement and make good pals. They can enjoy many satisfying marathons where sex is akin to running a race. Mars in Leo is a compelling, intriguing lover since he shares Gemini's love of show, role-playing, and talking too much. Watching these two signs interact is like watching a stage production of *Peter Pan*. Plus, there's a bisexual element whenever Gemini is involved. The Leo man appeals to Gemini since he loves to preen and prance.

Mars Signs to Avoid Like the Plague: Mars in Capricorn is much too slow and conservative to satisfy Venus in Gemini sexually. He often lacks the finesse and imagination that Venus in Gemini requires in her lover. Mars in Taurus and Venus in Gemini may also be unhappily matched since Taurus is usually not sensitive enough to deal with the nervous neuroses commonly found in Gemini people.

VENUS IN CANCER

This alluring child of the Moon is very much the romantic, but it is difficult to associate the sexual aspect with shy Venus in Cancer. She seems too bashful and hesitant to initiate sex. Yet her intuitive powers make her an excellent sex partner. She is capable of great empathy and is willing to please her lover. Venus in Cancer is both dreamy and powerfully psychic. In many respects, she is the idealized woman since Cancer is considered one of the most feminine of all signs. True, she is statuesque with gorgeous breasts. Her complexion is often milky pale, her eyes large and unsure. This woman is vulnerable, but she is not weak. Far from it, Venus in Cancer can be tough as nails. Try to attack a member of her family and you'll see how strong she is!

    She can withstand a lot, but this woman is enormously compassionate and protective. Venus in Cancer has deep alternating layers in her personality. She can be as private and as difficult to know as a Scorpio. Rarely promiscuous, Venus in Cancer wants you to understand her soul before moving on to a sexual relationship. She's as romantic as a Tennessee Williams play, yet Venus in Cancer isn't an idiot. In fact, she can be quite coy.

Cancer can also be practical. This what divides her—good-old-fashioned common sense complicated by a hunger for romance and magic. Blanche DuBois (the protagonist in the famous Tennessee Williams play *A Streetcar Named Desire*) was a Cancer-Leo personality. She had all the drama and romance, the fantasies of passion and power, but this extreme vulnerability. Blanche also carried around a ratty suitcase, with all of her memories from the past intact. That's a Cancer for you. She holds on to things, and this includes emotional wounds. Don't hurt this woman. She seems fragile, but she won't fall apart. If you stray, however, rather than stay, she won't ever forgive you.

Most Compatible Mars Signs: Venus in Cancer and Mars in Scorpio can be the ideal match. Both are sensitive and passionate, with a dash of common sense often lacking in the other Water sign, Pisces. Love between these two signs can be deep, involving, and intense. The only word of caution is that both signs are subject to petty jealousies, which could sour this almost perfect match. Plus, Venus in Cancer rules the erogenous zone of the breasts, while Scorpio rules the genital area. What could be better? On the other hand, Mars in Pisces is an adept and slippery lover. He is psychic and intuitive just as Cancer is. When you throw a Mars in Pisces with a Venus in Cancer in the same room, it's not surprising that they end up in the sack.

Interesting Combos in Case You're Looking for Fireworks: Mars in Leo has an interesting variety of qualities to offer Venus in Cancer. Both are richly romantic signs. They exist side by side and have a number of traits in common—one of which is amplified emotions. Leo is just more overt about it. Another interesting love match would be Mars in Libra. This is the kind of gentle, adoring lover that insecure Venus in Cancer truly needs.

Mars Signs to Avoid Like the Plague: The Venus-in-Cancer woman should not be distracted or fooled by the Mars-in-Aries man. He is rugged and fascinating; however, the Mars-in-Aries man can never truly appreciate the exquisite, honed sensitivity of a Cancer. He may try to unlock the mystery of this watery Venus sign, but the fact of the matter is, he never will. He is too busy competing with her and others to truly understand her. Venus in Cancer should steer clear of Mars in Capricorn, too. After getting to know her, he'll probably be tabulating her yearly income in his head.

VENUS IN LEO

If you remember the screen legend Mae West, she was the quintessential Leo woman. Venus in Leo is warm, she loves to purr, and she always goes in for dramatics. Venus feels comfortable in the sign of Leo since this sign gives artistic talent, finesse, and impeccable taste to a horoscope chart. The Venus-in-Leo woman can be rather vain, and no wonder, since her physical appearance is typically quite stunning. The sexual component in this woman's chart is her own image or her ego. Don't get me wrong, she's not shallow; but her lovers must flatter her—always. It's not that Venus in Leo expects to be number one, she simply wants to rise above the crowd.

What is erotic for this woman is the way *she* appears to herself in the mirror. Keeping her image up is vital and when her looks fail her, she can become grumpy and very depressed. The image Venus in Leo projects means everything. She must find her own self "arousing" before she allows her lovers to look at her in the same way. She has a strong sense of beauty, which is often embellished and quite elaborate.

Venus in Leo tends to use her lovers as mirrors, and the more handsome or rich they are reflects well on her. This dramatic sign reads her own image in her lover's eyes and responds to that. This is of critical importance to how the relationship progresses. The real truth is that she lacks esteem and sets high standards for herself. Leo just can't be "good enough," so she has to be above the minions. Remember to tell her how beautiful she is—always— and you'll get along just fine.

Most Compatible Mars Signs: Mars in Sagittarius equals the creative energies of Venus in Leo, not to mention the need to explore new territories and experiences—naturally, this also applies sexually. When Venus in Leo tires of this rather ordinary guy, however, her attentions turn to Mars in Aries, whose aggressive energies she finds quite arousing. Mars in Aries can take Venus to the heights of passion, but when coupled for a period of time, she can also expect power plays and ego conflicts.

Interesting Combos in Case You're Looking for Fireworks: Mars in Taurus has a strong sexual appetite and can bring Venus in Leo many hours of passion. These two signs "square" each other, meaning both are fixed signs, so there will be certain tensions that will add excitement to the relationship. Her most compelling lover, however, is a man born with his Mars in Scorpio. Scorpio's Rasputin-like charisma and his sexual focus on Venus in Leo is flattering at first—that is, until she finds out how possessive and jealous he is. If the jealousy aspect can be worked out, their sex life can be delicious and mutually satisfying for many years.

Mars Signs to Avoid Like the Plague: With the exception of Mars in Scorpio, water signs seldom appeal to Venus in Leo. Sex between Venus in Leo and Mars in Pisces usually creates little more than hot air and dissipating steam. Sex with Mars in Cancer, who wants his lover to also be his mother, can seem infantile and neurotic to lusty Leo. Mars in Capricorn is less than ideal. Ruled by Saturn, Capricorn is sometimes an icy sign. Mars in Capricorn can also indicate difficulties with women.

VENUS IN VIRGO

Often shy and self-effacing, the Venus-in-Virgo woman still has no trouble attracting lovers. We see aspects of her in every culture— the archetype of Venus as goddess of love and growth, who is often represented as a virgin. *The Birth of Venus*, by Florentine artist Sandro Botticelli, best portrays the nubile virgin goddess rising from the waves and being carried to shore on half a seashell, where dancing muses await in the lush, dark greenery. Botticelli's green is not the pale green of spring or the bright green of early summer. His greenery is dark, enclosed, and mature, the kind found in late summer when the Sun, Mercury, and Venus slide into the sign of the Virgin. It is the green of renewal, planet-power, and growth.

It is strange that we have named this sign "Virgo." She is not always so pure. Gentle, to be sure, Venus in Virgo can at times be uninterested in sex; but more commonly, she leans toward being promiscuous. The sexual aspect of various signs is a well-known fact but is seldom uttered about Virgo. Venus in Virgo is demure, that is for sure. She enjoys exploring taboos while no one is looking. Under the yoke of society's mores, she rebels against it all undercover. Venus in Virgo does not want her pristine reputation tarnished! She doesn't want to seem like a bad girl, even when she acts like one—all in secret, of course. That's when you get her "sugar wouldn't melt in her mouth" facade, but, Oh, Baby, under the covers—only her lover knows for sure. Venus in Virgo sometimes likes to steal sex or kisses with her best friend's husband or boyfriend. Since Virgo is still a puritan at heart, it can all get a bit kinky. The next day, she'll pretend she doesn't know the guy, with eyes averted, when she passes him on the street. Don't get me wrong. Venus in Virgo never acts on impulse and, according to her, she makes no mistakes. Complex and into sexual strategy, she plays her love life like a game of chess.

Most Compatible Mars Signs: Placid Mars in Taurus promises Venus in Virgo many hours of sensual pleasure. Both are practical and tolerant of each other's needs. Lovemaking tends to be luxurious and relaxed with these signs. In fact, they become so used to each other, they finish each other's sentences. Mars in Capricorn shares the same no-nonsense attitude in the bedroom.

Interesting Combos in Case You're Looking for Fireworks: Mars in Gemini knows how to tickle her funny bone and her fancy. These signs are equally fickle and have much in common, including their neuroses. They are both mutable signs and love word and trivia games, exhibiting a chameleon-like quality that makes them equals and versatile lovers. Mars in Pisces will reach into the depths of Venus in Virgo's soul. There is a bond, whereby Pisces can awaken in Virgo qualities she didn't know were there.

Mars Signs to Avoid Like the Plague: Mars in Aries comes on too strong for Virgo—so much so that it would be highly unusual for these two signs to be attracted to each other at all. It is unlikely that this Mars-ruled ruffian would ever satisfy Virgo's undying need to feel loved. Another sign quite incompatible with Virgo is Aquarius. Mars in Aquarius doesn't play by the rules, especially sexually. Venus in Virgo would be turned off by someone she considers a sexual anarchist or just an everyday wacked-out weirdo.

VENUS IN LIBRA

Just call her *Venus De Milo*. This woman inspires all guys to start crooning, "You are soooo beautiful . . . too . . . meeee." There's no doubt about it. Venus in Libra is a drop-dead gorgeous sign who grabs attention wherever she goes, but she is never overt about hogging the attention. Venus, the planet of beauty, is exalted in Libra. You hardly ever run across an ugly Libra. Nearly all Librans are attractive. Even the ugly ones are quite talented at making themselves look better. Looks are important to Libra and this can be her downfall. She goes for charmers and hunks, rather than wise men, which is often a mistake.

Libra is a sign that forms sudden attachments. Her mind is almost always wrapped in the fantasy of a romance. We call Libra "the marrying sign," because, for better or worse, Libra believes that a romance, or a marriage to the right man, will solve all of her problems. In this day and age, most of us realize that this isn't true, but Libra holds on. Come hell or high water, Venus in Libra will keep her man. What is so surprising is that this woman is often stunning to look at. She could have any man she desires. Then she snaps up the first bum that comes along. Venus in Libra doesn't care. He's breathing, isn't he? This delusional belief is the source of most of her problems. For a woman so bent on marriage, this is one area of her life where she fails a lot. Sexually, Libra is an attentive, adoring lover. The trouble with Venus in

Libra is that she needs to take a firm stand and not accept the first man who asks her to slow dance as "good enough to tango." She needs to know that the right guy is the one worth waiting for.

Most Compatible Mars Signs: Mars in Gemini loves the way this woman flirts since he also adores sexual teasing. Mars in Aquarius has the kind of mind that fascinates and enthralls Venus in Libra. He uses his encyclopedia of unusual facts to woo and entertain his lover before making a first move. There must be an intellectual component to all of her relationships because she is exceptionally smart.

Interesting Combos in Case You're Looking for Fireworks: Mars in Aries spells *danger* to Venus in Libra. She often becomes infatuated with the devil-may-care-come-what-may Aries type. Fiery Mars is even more assertive and direct when it falls in the sign of Aries.

Mars Signs to Avoid Like the Plague: Mars in Pisces lacks the direction and passion that Venus in Libra seeks. Mars in Capricorn could provide the material possessions that Venus in Libra requires, but this sign tends to be rather aloof and often has difficulties with women. A man or woman of any sign who is crude or off-color will immediately turn off the Venus-in-Libra woman.

VENUS IN SCORPIO

She is mysterious. She is dazzling. She has the slinky energy of a sleek black cat. Men find this woman charismatic, compelling, and they will go to the ends of the earth, even to hell, to win her love and win her sex. No matter that Venus in Scorpio is paranoid and controlling. No matter that she has some other poor sucker dangling on a string. It feels so damned good while it lasts. This woman has all kinds of power, and she wants to own you—mind, body, and soul. She has an amorous, romantic spirit, and there's an added bonus—she *loves* sex.

Venus in Scorpio likes to flirt and play, but she doesn't want you to do the same. She is ruled by her passions and desires to love with wild abandonment. Often, though, she holds back and then envies others who aren't afraid to explore the uncharted territories of sexual love. She swings between being a puritan and a femme fatale. It's no surprise that World War I spy Mata Hari was a Scorpio. (After all, Scorpio is the sign of the spy.) And it's no surprise that she ended up dying for her passions and her indiscretions.

Thus, the Venus-in-Scorpio woman is afraid of surrendering to her passions. She knows she has vulnerabilities and fears she'll drown in them. It takes a while to win this woman's trust. She views everyone as either a possible ally or an enemy. If she considers you an enemy, you can kiss your sex life goodbye. Although highly sexual, Scorpio can be celibate a long time. There is no in-between; there are only extremes. So, love Venus in Scorpio gently and with understanding. After all, she's the most passionate sign of all.

Most Compatible Mars Signs: Mars in Cancer is the one sign that gains the Venus-in-Scorpio woman's trust. Scorpio feels that Cancer is sensitive and patient. He also understands the jealousy and possessiveness of Venus in Scorpio because he's somewhat that way himself—although not to such an extreme degree. Mars in Pisces makes Venus in Scorpio feel cherished. This Mars sign may need to learn to stand up for his own needs and interests, however, instead of bowing down and kowtowing to the Queen of Sex.

Interesting Combos in Case You're Looking for Fireworks: Allow me to fill you in on a delicious secret. The best lover a Venus in Scorpio woman can find is a man who has his Mars in Scorpio. Sexually, they fit as nicely together as a hand in a velvet glove. Don't expect the relationship to last much longer than the sex, but if it does, learn to respect your lover's need for privacy and occasional freedom. All good things require sacrifice. I don't have to tell you *that*, now do I, Scorpio? Another satisfying sex partner for Venus in Scorpio is a man with his Mars in Leo. This man enjoys the intrigue and passion of a Scorpio and will be loyal as long as she abstains from trying to control him.

Mars Signs to Avoid Like the Plague: If Venus in Scorpio is hankering for an ulcer, she'll need to try a man with his Mars in Sagittarius. This man is completely unpredictable and impossible to control. These are traits Scorpio loathes in a person. Also, this guy is very sociable; he likes to party hardy with the boys and girls and a lampshade on his head. Venus in Scorpio's high-strung nerves couldn't take this man for too long. He'll think they're having fun, but she'll see it for what it is—her view of, well, *hell*. Another bad match is a man with his Mars in Aries. He must always be in control, as well, but you can't have two people driving a car at the same time.

VENUS IN SAGITTARIUS

She's playful and she's funny. She likes to flirt, but she's really not too serious. Basically, the Venus in Sagittarius is a joy to be around. She's warm, curious, and endlessly sensual. She can be a flattering lover since she asks lots of questions and is interested in a variety of topics. Venus in Sagittarius is not a terribly monogamous sign, though. After she gets married, she soon realizes that marriage is a social convention that makes her miserable—and when she becomes miserable, she makes her spouse miserable. This is a sign who should definitely not marry too young. Venus in Sagittarius begins to wonder what she's missed, and that's when she begins looking at the other stallions—especially the ones who act like Jeff Foxworthy—because let's face it, he is her ideal type. In general, Sagittarius likes anyone who likes her first. She isn't too picky because she sees worth in just about everyone. Venus in Sagittarius doesn't go for the most handsome guy; she goes for the one who can make her laugh the most. She's not judgmental and actually likes silliness. In fact, a person's difference is often what initially attracts her.

Then there are those "parties" she throws. Any occasion is good enough for this girl to break into a party—as long as there are two people and the other one is you. The nice thing about having a relationship with Venus in Sagittarius is you don't have to be perfect, just as long as you are fun to be around. She takes sex rather casually and very seldom falls victim to lower impulses such as revenge, hate, or jealousy. The only sour note is that most of her attractions and love affairs are not enduring. She has a taste for the new and different—and she tends to go for one-night stands. Naturally, this often means changing lovers in midstream. But change is good, especially when it comes to Venus in Sagittarius.

Most Compatible Mars Signs: Sagittarius is a lively sign, usually quite extroverted, and the same could be said for fire-breathing Leo. It would seem only natural that a Venus in Sagittarius could achieve sexual harmony with Mars in Leo, since he is as fond of dramatics as she is. Because of pride and a need to impress, Mars in Leo is attractive to the Venus in Sagittarius woman. Leo does not want his lover to have any reason to think less of him and he will work hard to gain her approval. Mars in Aries also is a formidable lover since he likes to come out on top no matter what the circumstances are. Both signs are passionate and eager to please. Only these fiery signs can match the flames of freedom of a Venus in Sagittarius woman.

Interesting Combos in Case You're Looking for Fireworks: If Venus in Sagittarius is in the mood for fun and doesn't mind verbal sparring before the relationship gets serious, the Mars in Gemini man will provide lots of laughs and some interesting diversions for her. The Mars in Aquarius man is rebellious and rather odd, and able to show Venus in Sagittarius things she's never seen or experienced before. Aquarius is the sign of the anarchist. An Aquarius can always top a Sagittarius when it comes to acts of cultural or personal rebellion and this *fascinates* her!

Mars Signs to Avoid Like the Plague: Mars in Taurus moves slowly and Venus in Sagittarius moves fast. Get the picture? These two signs would endlessly frustrate each other. Also, Mars in Taurus generally does not find a Sagittarius particularly charming. In fact, he thinks her fickle and completely lacking in common sense. What about that other mutable sign, Mars in Virgo? Mars in Virgo doesn't think Venus in Sagittarius is too funny, either, but is usually polite, if not aloof, about the whole issue.

Venus in Capricorn

Just call her Billy Goat Gruff. She can be pleasant when she wants to be but in a dry, understated way. She is a no-nonsense person and is extremely level headed—that is, unless Venus in Capricorn becomes power-drunk, and then she loses all of the common sense she is so proud of. When it comes to love and sex, issues such as money, status, or social standing are much more important to her. If you check into her past, you will find that this woman probably felt a lack of some sort—perhaps emotional coldness from one or both parents. Conditioning from this austere, emotional environment taught Venus in Capricorn that practical matters come first.

This woman doesn't enter love affairs too easily. She doesn't want to be bothered by something that diverts her mind from her key goal of making money, gaining power, or scratching her way to the top. All other matters take a back seat. Her lovers must have the potential for making lots of money or gaining status. More than any other sign, Capricorn considers power the ultimate aphrodisiac. Of course, this can be true in all signs, but with Venus in Capricorn it is especially true. She wants a man of influence, a regular V.I.P. Otherwise, she's not interested.

Occasionally, the Venus in Capricorn does make the mistake of dating a no-good bum, but if she does, it's usually because he's a con artist who uses "big talk" that has to do with money or status and thereby appeals to her need for power or influence. This woman can be deceived by her hunger for the grandiose. She requires moral strength from a lover, a winner in terms of the rat race, and a genuine commitment toward a shared future. When you meet her requirements, Venus in Capricorn will be yours forever.

Most Compatible Mars Signs: Mars in Taurus sings the same tune as Venus in Capricorn—they both want to look important to their community and their friends. Taurus is also an empathetic, sensual lover who can draw Venus in Capricorn out of her shell. If anyone can meet her needs for both "things" and sex, Mars in Taurus is the man for the job. Mars in Virgo is patient with Venus in Capricorn and understands her sexual aloofness, but lovemaking between these two signs, though good in the beginning, can often go stale for lack of imagination.

Interesting Combos in Case You're Looking for Fireworks: Fireworks? What about rocket ships? Venus in Capricorn may want to link up with Mars in Aquarius. This is a sign that can take her flying to other planets. That is, if she survives him. This Angel of the Odd would have Venus in Capricorn in a constant state of frustration. The sensitivity of Mars in Cancer can provide the kind of nurturing the Venus in Capricorn woman desperately needs. Mars in Cancer can relate to the practical interests, and also worries, of Venus in Capricorn, while using strength and wisdom to alleviate her fears and insecurities.

Mars Signs to Avoid Like the Plague: Mars in Gemini and Mars in Sagittarius are both unsettling signs for Venus in Capricorn. Their need to "wing it" through life, while seeking out the shocking or unexpected, would send Venus in Capricorn straight for the psychiatrist's couch. After all, Venus in Capricorn looks for security in her life, not shocks and weird surprises.

VENUS IN AQUARIUS

Venus in Aquarius is a citizen of this world and others. She can visualize and imagine things that the rest of us can't. For this reason, Venus in Aquarius is looking for someone strange and radically different from the kind of partner her family expects her to have. After all, Aquarius does not want to seem ordinary in any way, shape, or form. Sometimes this means dating outside her race or place of ethnic origin. Venus in Aquarius is searching for someone who treats her as the unique individual she really is. She wants her lover to show her things, ways of life and sex, she hasn't seen or experienced before.

She isn't looking for a traditional family life. She doesn't want to be a hausfrau in a little cottage with a white picket fence. In fact, what she really wants is to live on Venus and Mars, to experience love in the stars. She wants to be sent into orbit on a rocket ship. It goes without saying that this woman is not easy to please. She must be friends with her lovers first. Romance, if it ever truly surfaces in its traditional form, will certainly not be typical. Generally, Aquarius is not a romantic sign by nature, but she is certainly not practical either.

She likes to share "a cause," a visionary quest with her lover, as sexual friends of the opposite sex working toward some common goal. If you like the untried and unique, this woman is for you. If traditional values of hearth, country, and home are your games, it would be wise to leave this smart cookie alone. If the mind is your game, however, and you want a cause, you might consider following this idealistic gypsy to the ends of the universe.

Most Compatible Mars Signs: Mars in Gemini shares many of the same ideals as Venus in Aquarius; they're just a bit more fickle. The mental and sexual dexterity of Mars in Gemini is appealing to androgynous Venus in Aquarius. Mars in Libra also exhibits the same sense of fairness and the ability to keep his mind and opinions open. In this way, these two dual signs, Gemini and Libra, are willing to experiment in the taboo areas of sex that Venus in Aquarius is so curious about.

Interesting Combos in Case You're Looking for Fireworks: Mars in Leo attracts attention, and Venus in Aquarius finds this exciting. Although Venus in Aquarius dares to be different, Mars in Leo is the one who can put on the pomp and circumstance. These opposite signs have much to admire in each other since neither one minds "being on display." In fact, they rather like it. Thus, sex in inappropriate places is a fun diversion from their routine. It takes the smoldering, magic wand of the Leo man to put some sexual fire in Venus in Aquarius' tail.

Mars Signs to Avoid Like the Plague: Mars in Capricorn is the worst because he lacks the kind of imagination or desire for fantasy in the bedroom that Venus in Aquarius seeks. The next worst match for her is Mars in Cancer. This sign prefers to live in the past, even in the bedroom. Venus in Aquarius finds the past generally boring unless, of course, you are talking about the Middle Ages, the Vikings, or something a little weird. Venus in Aquarius needs to steer clear of boring people of any sign.

VENUS IN PISCES

She's a starry-eyed romantic or a gullible guppy—depending upon your perspective. Not only does it depend upon *your* perspective, it depends on *hers* as well. The problem is, Venus in Pisces is a reflection of the people she is around. If her friends are decent and positive, she will be as well. If her friends are glue-sniffers or ax-murderers—well, you get the picture.

Venus in Pisces is different. She is spiritual, having the highest laws of the universe imprinted on her soul. She understands the deeper, more spiritual dimensions of romantic love. She has high ideals. It's just that she rarely lives up to them. Venus in

Pisces absorbs vibrations the way a sieve soaks up water. Everything goes through her, affecting her briefly, and then there is another change. Pisces is a timeless ocean of possibility, or someone with a history of hard luck headed down a dead-end street. It all depends upon who her friends are.

Venus in Pisces is mystical and super-sensitive, but this doesn't mean she is innocent. It doesn't mean Venus in Pisces doesn't have experience. In truth, Pisces can be one of the most promiscuous signs of all, because she doesn't know where she ends and where her lover begins. Venus in Pisces, though sweet and kind, can be rather vague about her own identity. This is probably the greatest plight of Pisces, sign of the Double Fishes. She is often ignorant of who she truly is, looking for clues in her lover's eyes. Yet there is no sign quite as alluring, charismatic, and sensual as the woman with Venus in Pisces.

She needs to know that her sensitivity and ability to give love are her strengths and not weaknesses. When her needs are met, Pisces is the most loving life partner of all the signs. As long as the relationship remains honest and Pisces isn't afraid to be who she really is, you can get lost, but not drown, in her oceans of love.

Most Compatible Mars Signs: What about Venus in Pisces with Mars in Scorpio? No doubt about it—this is a soulmate connection. Think of the attraction that once was between Elizabeth Taylor and Richard Burton. They represent the alluring energies between the signs of Pisces and Scorpio. These two signs can't get enough of each other, and this is especially true when Mars is in Scorpio and Venus is in Pisces. Both signs are inordinately sensitive and revel in oceans of sex and emotional depth. When these two signs meet, *it's the real thing*. Another good match for Venus in Pisces is intuitive Mars in Cancer. Mars in Cancer can be a strong and sensitive, slightly feminine man—not necessarily in a homosexual way, but in a very sweet, protective way. Venus in Pisces loves and *needs* to have a leader, to have a father or a mother. Mars in Cancer is the best sign to provide this. Plus, this relationship is not as likely to take a negative turn since Mars in Cancer is patient and understands Pisces' problems.

Interesting Combos in Case You're Looking for Fireworks: The logical selection would be Pisces' opposite sign, Virgo, except that it isn't necessarily true. Pisces and Virgo share many talents, but also some of the same weaknesses. They are both overly sensitive signs and lack a backbone, to be perfectly honest. For fireworks, Venus in Pisces needs to try a Mars in Leo man. Both love drama and passionate romance. Leo is ostentatious, but Pisces likes costuming and drama, too, although she is a little more understated. Both signs tend to be fantasy-prone.

Mars Signs to Avoid Like the Plague: Venus in Pisces needs to seriously avoid a relationship with Mars in Aries. Oftentimes, side-by-side zodiac signs, like Pisces and Aries, may share some traits, like a brother-and-sister team. In this case, it is rarely true. Mars in Aries and Venus in Pisces are absolutely antithetical to each other. Aries simply doesn't comprehend Pisces and views her as terribly weak. Plus, Piscean vulnerability brings out the sadistic streak in Aries, which is always present. For Aries, it should be all up-front, obvious, and ready for truth-or-dare, but Pisces people thrive on emotional nuances and vibes. In most cases, Aries is baffled by and judgmental of the unusual sensitivity of Pisces, which Aries sees as sick or dysfunctional. Pisces in her most positive state, however, is what Aries cannot be—tough as nails and truly kind.

VENUS TABLES FROM 1935-2000

The following are sign positions for the planet Venus from 1935 until 2000. Venus stays in a sign for as little as four weeks or for as long as four months. The dates listed below are the days upon which seductive Venus changes into a new guise, or sign. For instance, if you were born on April 22, 1970, your Venus sign would be in Taurus. Venus did not move into the sign of Gemini until April 27.

Here's a trickier one. What if you were born on October 11, 1970? On September 7 Venus entered the sign Scorpio. Venus stayed in Scorpio until January 7, 1971, when it changed into Sagittarius. So what is the Venus sign for October 11?

Scorpio. October 11 falls between the dates of September 7 and January 7. The date listed is when the Venus sign begins. The date that follows is when the sign changes.

(PLEASE NOTE: When a planet seems to dip back into the previous sign, it is in what is called a "retrograde motion." This simply means that, from earth, Venus or Mars appears to have moved back into the previous sign for a few weeks. Simply look up your birth date and see in what sign it falls. Even if the planet is "retrograde" it is still in the sign described. Unless you are interested in learning advanced astrology, you needn't worry about retrogrades.)

1935

January 8 Venus in Aquarius

February 1 Venus in Pisces

February 26 Venus in Aries

March 22 Venus in Taurus

April 16 Venus in Gemini

May 11 Venus in Cancer

June 7 Venus in Leo

July 7 Venus in Virgo

November 9 Venus in Libra

December 8 Venus in Scorpio

1936

January 3 Venus in Sagittarius
January 28 Venus in Capricorn
February 22 Venus in Aquarius
March 17 Venus in Pisces
April 11 Venus in Aries
May 5 Venus in Taurus
May 29 Venus in Gemini
June 23 Venus in Cancer
July 17 Venus in Leo
August 11 Venus in Virgo
September 4 Venus in Libra
September 28 Venus in Scorpio
October 23 Venus in Sagittarius
November 16 Venus in Capricorn
December 11 Venus in Aquarius

1937

January 6 Venus in Pisces
February 2 Venus in Aries
March 9 Venus in Taurus
April 14 Venus in Aries
June 4 Venus in Taurus
July 7 Venus in Gemini
August 4 Venus in Cancer
August 31 Venus in Leo
September 25 Venus in Virgo
October 19 Venus in Libra
November 12 Venus in Scorpio
December 6 Venus in Sagittarius
December 30 Venus in Capricorn

1938

January 23 Venus in Aquarius
February 16 Venus in Pisces

March 12 Venus in Aries
April 5 Venus in Taurus
April 29 Venus in Gemini
May 24 Venus in Cancer
June 18 Venus in Leo
July 14 Venus in Virgo
August 9 Venus in Libra
September 7 Venus in Scorpio
October 13 Venus in Sagittarius
November 15 Venus in Scorpio

1939

January 4 Venus in Sagittarius
February 6 Venus in Capricorn
March 5 Venus in Aquarius
March 31 Venus in Pisces
April 25 Venus in Aries
May 20 Venus in Taurus
June 14 Venus in Gemini
July 9 Venus in Cancer
August 2 Venus in Leo
August 26 Venus in Virgo
September 20 Venus in Libra
October 14 Venus in Scorpio
November 7 Venus in Sagittarius
December 1 Venus in Capricorn
December 25 Venus in Aquarius

1940

January 18 Venus in Pisces
February 12 Venus in Aries
March 8 Venus in Taurus
April 4 Venus in Gemini
May 6 Venus in Cancer
July 5 Venus in Gemini

August 1 Venus in Cancer
September 8 Venus in Leo
October 6 Venus in Virgo
November 1 Venus in Libra
November 26 Venus in Scorpio
December 20 Venus in Sagittarius

1941

January 13 Venus in Capricorn
February 12 Venus in Aquarius
March 2 Venus in Pisces
March 27 Venus in Aries
April 20 Venus in Taurus
May 14 Venus in Gemini
June 7 Venus in Cancer
July 2 Venus in Leo
August 21 Venus in Libra
September 15 Venus in Scorpio
October 10 Venus in Sagittarius
November 6 Venus in Capricorn
December 5 Venus in Aquarius

1942

April 6 Venus in Pisces
May 6 Venus in Aries
June 2 Venus in Taurus
June 27 Venus in Gemini
July 23 Venus in Cancer
August 17 Venus in Leo
September 10 Venus in Virgo
October 4 Venus in Libra
October 28 Venus in Scorpio
November 21 Venus in Sagittarius
December 15 Venus in Capricorn

1943

January 8 Venus in Aquarius
February 1 Venus in Pisces
February 25 Venus in Aries
March 21 Venus in Taurus
April 15 Venus in Gemini
May 11 Venus in Cancer
June 7 Venus in Leo
July 7 Venus in Virgo
November 9 Venus in Libra
December 8 Venus in Scorpio

1944

January 3 Venus in Sagittarius
January 28 Venus in Capricorn
February 21 Venus in Aquarius
March 17 Venus in Pisces
April 10 Venus in Aries
May 4 Venus in Taurus
May 29 Venus in Gemini
June 22 Venus in Cancer
July 17 Venus in Leo
August 10 Venus in Virgo
September 3 Venus in Libra
September 28 Venus in Scorpio
October 22 Venus in Sagittarius
November 16 Venus in Capricorn
December 11 Venus in Aquarius

1945

January 5 Venus in Pisces
February 2 Venus in Aries
March 11 Venus in Taurus
April 7 Venus in Aries
June 4 Venus in Taurus

July 7 Venus in Gemini
August 4 Venus in Cancer
August 30 Venus in Leo
September 24 Venus in Virgo
October 19 Venus in Libra
November 12 Venus in Scorpio
December 6 Venus in Sagittarius
December 30 Venus in Capricorn

1946

January 22 Venus in Aquarius
February 15 Venus in Pisces
March 11 Venus in Aries
April 5 Venus in Taurus
April 29 Venus in Gemini
May 24 Venus in Cancer
June 18 Venus in Leo
July 13 Venus in Virgo
August 9 Venus in Libra
September 7 Venus in Scorpio
October 6 Venus in Sagittarius
November 9 Venus in Scorpio

1947

January 5 Venus in Sagittarius
February 6 Venus in Capricorn
March 5 Venus in Aquarius
March 30 Venus in Pisces
April 25 Venus in Aries
May 20 Venus in Taurus
June 13 Venus in Gemini
July 8 Venus in Cancer
August 2 Venus in Leo
August 26 Venus in Virgo

September 19 Venus in Libra
October 13 Venus in Scorpio
November 6 Venus in Sagittarius
November 30 Venus in Capricorn
December 24 Venus in Aquarius

1948

January 18 Venus in Pisces
February 11 Venus in Aries
March 8 Venus in Taurus
April 4 Venus in Gemini
May 7 Venus in Cancer
June 29 Venus in Gemini
August 3 Venus in Cancer
September 8 Venus in Leo
October 6 Venus in Virgo
November 1 Venus in Libra
November 26 Venus in Scorpio
December 20 Venus in Sagittarius

1949

January 13 Venus in Capricorn
February 6 Venus in Aquarius
March 2 Venus in Pisces
March 26 Venus in Aries
April 19 Venus in Taurus
May 14 Venus in Gemini
June 7 Venus in Cancer
July 1 Venus in Leo
July 26 Venus in Virgo
August 20 Venus in Libra
September 14 Venus in Scorpio
October 10 Venus in Sagittarius
November 6 Venus in Capricorn
December 6 Venus in Aquarius

1950

April 6 Venus in Pisces
May 5 Venus in Aries
June 1 Venus in Taurus
June 27 Venus in Gemini
July 22 Venus in Cancer
August 16 Venus in Leo
September 10 Venus in Virgo
October 4 Venus in Libra
October 28 Venus in Scorpio
November 21 Venus in Sagittarius
December 14 Venus in Capricorn

1951

January 7 Venus in Aquarius
January 31 Venus in Pisces
February 24 Venus in Aries
March 21 Venus in Taurus
April 15 Venus in Gemini
May 11 Venus in Cancer
June 7 Venus in Leo
July 8 Venus in Virgo
November 9 Venus in Libra
December 8 Venus in Scorpio

1952

January 2 Venus in Sagittarius
January 27 Venus in Capricorn
February 21 Venus in Aquarius
March 16 Venus in Pisces
April 9 Venus in Aries
May 4 Venus in Taurus
May 28 Venus in Gemini
June 22 Venus in Cancer
July 16 Venus in Leo

August 9 Venus in Virgo
September 3 Venus in Libra
September 27 Venus in Scorpio
October 22 Venus in Sagittarius
November 12 Venus in Capricorn
December 10 Venus in Aquarius

1953

January 5 Venus in Pisces
February 2 Venus in Aries
March 14 Venus in Taurus
March 31 Venus in Aries
June 5 Venus in Taurus
July 7 Venus in Gemini
August 4 Venus in Cancer
August 30 Venus in Leo
September 24 Venus in Virgo
October 18 Venus in Libra
November 11 Venus in Scorpio
December 5 Venus in Sagittarius
December 29 Venus in Capricorn

1954

January 22 Venus in Aquarius
February 15 Venus in Pisces
March 11 Venus in Aries
April 4 Venus in Taurus
April 28 Venus in Gemini
May 23 Venus in Cancer
June 17 Venus in Leo
July 13 Venus in Virgo
August 9 Venus in Libra
September 7 Venus in Scorpio
October 23 Venus in Sagittarius
October 27 Venus in Scorpio

1955

January 6 Venus in Sagittarius
February 6 Venus in Capricorn
March 4 Venus in Aquarius
March 30 Venus in Pisces
April 24 Venus in Aries
May 19 Venus in Taurus
June 13 Venus in Gemini
July 8 Venus in Cancer
August 1 Venus in Leo
August 25 Venus in Virgo
September 18 Venus in Libra
October 13 Venus in Scorpio
November 6 Venus in Sagittarius
November 30 Venus in Capricorn
December 24 Venus in Aquarius

1956

January 17 Venus in Pisces
February 11 Venus in Aries
March 7 Venus in Taurus
April 4 Venus in Gemini
May 8 Venus in Cancer
June 23 Venus in Gemini
August 4 Venus in Cancer
September 8 Venus in Leo
October 6 Venus in Virgo
October 21 Venus in Libra
November 25 Venus in Scorpio
December 19 Venus in Sagittarius

1957

January 12 Venus in Capricorn
February 5 Venus in Aquarius

March 1 Venus in Pisces
March 25 Venus in Aries
April 19 Venus in Taurus
May 13 Venus in Gemini
June 6 Venus in Cancer
July 1 Venus in Leo
July 26 Venus in Virgo
August 20 Venus in Libra
September 14 Venus in Scorpio
October 10 Venus in Sagittarius
November 5 Venus in Capricorn
December 6 Venus in Aquarius

1958

April 6 Venus in Pisces
May 5 Venus in Aries
June 1 Venus in Taurus
June 26 Venus in Gemini
July 22 Venus in Cancer
August 16 Venus in Leo
September 9 Venus in Virgo
October 3 Venus in Libra
October 27 Venus in Scorpio
November 20 Venus in Sagittarius
December 14 Venus in Capricorn

1959

January 7 Venus in Aquarius
January 31 Venus in Pisces
February 24 Venus in Aries
March 20 Venus in Taurus
April 14 Venus in Gemini
May 10 Venus in Cancer
June 6 Venus in Leo

July 8 Venus in Virgo
September 20 Venus in Leo
September 25 Venus in Virgo
November 9 Venus in Libra
December 7 Venus in Scorpio

1960

January 2 Venus in Sagittarius
January 27 Venus in Capricorn
February 20 Venus in Aquarius
March 16 Venus in Pisces
April 9 Venus in Aries
May 3 Venus in Taurus
May 28 Venus in Gemini
June 21 Venus in Cancer
July 16 Venus in Leo
August 9 Venus in Virgo
September 2 Venus in Libra
September 27 Venus in Scorpio
October 21 Venus in Sagittarius
November 15 Venus in Capricorn
December 10 Venus in Aquarius

1961

January 5 Venus in Pisces
February 2 Venus in Aries
June 5 Venus in Taurus
July 7 Venus in Gemini
August 3 Venus in Cancer
August 29 Venus in Leo
September 23 Venus in Virgo
October 18 Venus in Libra
November 11 Venus in Scorpio
December 5 Venus in Sagittarius

December 29 Venus in Capricorn

1962

January 21 Venus in Aquarius
February 14 Venus in Pisces
March 10 Venus in Aries
April 3 Venus in Taurus
April 28 Venus in Gemini
May 23 Venus in Cancer
June 17 Venus in Leo
July 12 Venus in Virgo
August 8 Venus in Libra
September 7 Venus in Scorpio

1963

January 6 Venus in Sagittarius
February 5 Venus in Capricorn
March 4 Venus in Aquarius
March 30 Venus in Pisces
April 24 Venus in Aries
May 19 Venus in Taurus
June 12 Venus in Gemini
July 7 Venus in Cancer
July 31 Venus in Leo
August 25 Venus in Virgo
September 18 Venus in Libra
October 12 Venus in Scorpio
November 5 Venus in Sagittarius
November 29 Venus in Capricorn
December 23 Venus in Aquarius

1964

January 17 Venus in Pisces
February 10 Venus in Aries

March 7 Venus in Taurus
April 4 Venus in Gemini
May 9 Venus in Cancer
June 17 Venus in Gemini
August 5 Venus in Cancer
September 8 Venus in Leo
October 5 Venus in Virgo
October 31 Venus in Libra
November 25 Venus in Scorpio
December 19 Venus in Sagittarius

1965
January 12 Venus in Capricorn
February 5 Venus in Aquarius
March 1 Venus in Pisces
March 25 Venus in Aries
April 18 Venus in Taurus
May 12 Venus in Gemini
June 6 Venus in Cancer
June 30 Venus in Leo
July 25 Venus in Virgo
August 19 Venus in Libra
September 13 Venus in Scorpio
October 9 Venus in Sagittarius
November 5 Venus in Capricorn
December 7 Venus in Aquarius

1966
February 6 Venus in Capricorn
February 25 Venus in Aquarius
April 6 Venus in Pisces
May 5 Venus in Aries
May 31 Venus in Taurus
June 26 Venus in Gemini
July 21 Venus in Cancer
August 15 Venus in Leo

September 8 Venus in Virgo
October 3 Venus in Libra
October 27 Venus in Scorpio
November 29 Venus in Sagittarius
December 13 Venus in Capricorn

1967
January 6 Venus in Aquarius
January 30 Venus in Pisces
February 23 Venus in Aries
March 20 Venus in Taurus
April 14 Venus in Gemini
May 10 Venus in Cancer
June 6 Venus in Leo
July 8 Venus in Virgo
September 9 Venus in Leo
October 1 Venus in Virgo
November 9 Venus in Libra
December 7 Venus in Scorpio

1968
January 1 Venus in Sagittarius
January 26 Venus in Capricorn
February 20 Venus in Aquarius
March 15 Venus in Pisces
April 8 Venus in Aries
May 3 Venus in Taurus
May 27 Venus in Gemini
June 21 Venus in Cancer
July 15 Venus in Leo
August 8 Venus in Virgo
September 2 Venus in Libra
September 26 Venus in Scorpio
October 21 Venus in Sagittarius
November 14 Venus in Capricorn
December 9 Venus in Aquarius

1969
January 4 Venus in Pisces
February 2 Venus in Aries
June 6 Venus in Taurus
July 6 Venus in Gemini
August 3 Venus in Cancer
August 29 Venus in Leo
September 23 Venus in Virgo
October 17 Venus in Libra
November 10 Venus in Scorpio
December 4 Venus in Sagittarius
December 28 Venus in Capricorn

1970
January 21 Venus in Aquarius
February 14 Venus in Pisces
March 10 Venus in Aries
April 3 Venus in Taurus
April 27 Venus in Gemini
May 22 Venus in Cancer
June 16 Venus in Leo
July 12 Venus in Virgo
August 8 Venus in Libra
September 7 Venus in Scorpio

1971
January 7 Venus in Sagittarius
February 5 Venus in Capricorn
March 4 Venus in Aquarius
March 29 Venus in Pisces
April 23 Venus in Aries
May 18 Venus in Taurus
June 12 Venus in Gemini
July 6 Venus in Cancer
July 31 Venus in Leo

August 24 Venus in Virgo
September 17 Venus in Libra
October 11 Venus in Scorpio
November 5 Venus in Sagittarius
November 29 Venus in Capricorn
December 23 Venus in Aquarius

1972
January 16 Venus in Pisces
February 10 Venus in Aries
March 7 Venus in Taurus
April 3 Venus in Gemini
May 10 Venus in Cancer
June 11 Venus in Gemini
August 6 Venus in Cancer
September 7 Venus in Leo
October 5 Venus in Virgo
October 30 Venus in Libra
November 24 Venus in Scorpio
December 18 Venus in Sagittarius

1973
January 11 Venus in Capricorn
February 4 Venus in Aquarius
March 24 Venus in Aries
April 18 Venus in Taurus
May 12 Venus in Gemini
June 5 Venus in Cancer
June 30 Venus in Leo
July 25 Venus in Virgo
August 19 Venus in Libra
September 13 Venus in Scorpio
October 9 Venus in Sagittarius
November 5 Venus in Capricorn
December 7 Venus in Aquarius

1974

January 29 Venus in Capricorn
February 28 Venus in Aquarius
April 6 Venus in Pisces
May 4 Venus in Aries
May 31 Venus in Taurus
June 25 Venus in Gemini
July 21 Venus in Cancer
August 14 Venus in Leo
September 8 Venus in Virgo
October 2 Venus in Libra
October 26 Venus in Scorpio
November 19 Venus in Sagittarius
December 13 Venus in Capricorn

1975

January 6 Venus in Aquarius
January 30 Venus in Pisces
February 23 Venus in Aries
March 19 Venus in Taurus
April 13 Venus in Gemini
May 9 Venus in Cancer
June 6 Venus in Leo
July 9 Venus in Virgo
September 2 Venus in Leo
October 4 Venus in Virgo
November 9 Venus in Libra
December 7 Venus in Scorpio

1976

January 1 Venus in Sagittarius
January 26 Venus in Capricorn
February 19 Venus in Aquarius
March 15 Venus in Pisces
April 8 Venus in Aries

May 2 Venus in Taurus
May 27 Venus in Gemini
June 20 Venus in Cancer
July 14 Venus in Leo
August 8 Venus in Virgo
September 1 Venus in Libra
September 26 Venus in Scorpio
October 20 Venus in Sagittarius
November 14 Capricorn
December 9 Venus in Aquarius

1977

January 4 Venus in Pisces
February 2 Venus in Aries
June 6 Venus in Taurus
July 6 Venus in Gemini
August 2 Venus in Cancer
August 28 Venus in Leo
September 22 Venus in Virgo
October 17 Venus in Libra
November 10 Venus in Scorpio
December 4 Venus in Sagittarius
December 27 Venus in Capricorn

1978

January 20 Venus in Aquarius
February 13 Venus in Pisces
March 9 Venus in Aries
April 2 Venus in Taurus
April 27 Venus in Gemini
May 22 Venus in Cancer
June 16 Venus in Leo
July 12 Venus in Virgo
August 8 Venus in Libra
September 7 Venus in Scorpio

1979

January 7 Venus in Sagittarius
February 5 Venus in Capricorn
March 3 Venus in Aquarius
March 29 Venus in Pisces
April 23 Venus in Aries
May 18 Venus in Taurus
June 11 Venus in Gemini
July 6 Venus in Cancer
July 30 Venus in Leo
August 24 Venus in Virgo
September 17 Venus in Libra
October 11 Venus in Scorpio
November 4 Venus in Sagittarius
November 28 Venus in Capricorn
December 22 Venus in Aquarius

1980

January 16 Venus in Pisces
February 9 Venus in Aries
March 6 Venus in Taurus
April 3 Venus in Gemini
May 12 Venus in Cancer
June 5 Venus in Gemini
August 6 Venus in Cancer
September 7 Venus in Leo
October 4 Venus in Virgo
October 30 Venus in Libra
November 24 Venus in Scorpio
December 18 Venus in Sagittarius

1981

January 11 Venus in Capricorn
February 4 Venus in Aquarius
February 28 Venus in Pisces

March 24 Venus in Aries
April 17 Venus in Taurus
May 11 Venus in Gemini
June 5 Venus in Cancer
June 29 Venus in Leo
July 24 Venus in Virgo
August 18 Venus in Libra
September 12 Venus in Scorpio
October 9 Venus in Sagittarius
November 5 Venus in Capricorn
December 8 Venus in Aquarius

1982

January 23 Venus in Capricorn
March 2 Venus in Aquarius
April 6 Venus in Pisces
May 4 Venus in Aries
May 30 Venus in Taurus
June 25 Venus in Gemini
July 20 Venus in Cancer
August 14 Venus in Leo
September 7 Venus in Virgo
October 2 Venus in Libra
October 26 Venus in Scorpio
November 18 Venus in Sagittarius
December 12 Venus in Capricorn

1983

January 5 Venus in Aquarius
January 29 Venus in Pisces
February 22 Venus in Aries
March 19 Venus in Taurus
April 13 Venus in Gemini
May 9 Venus in Cancer
June 6 Venus in Leo

July 10 Venus in Virgo
August 27 Venus in Leo
October 5 Venus in Virgo
November 9 Venus in Libra
December 6 Venus in Scorpio

1984

January 1 Venus in Sagittarius
January 25 Venus in Capricorn
February 19 Venus in Aquarius
March 14 Venus in Pisces
April 7 Venus in Aries
May 2 Venus in Taurus
May 26 Venus in Gemini
June 20 Venus in Cancer
July 14 Venus in Leo
August 7 Venus in Virgo
September 1 Venus in Libra
September 25 Venus in Scorpio
October 20 Venus in Sagittarius
November 13 Venus in Capricorn
December 9 Venus in Aquarius

1985

January 4 Venus in Pisces
February 2 Venus in Aries
June 6 Venus in Taurus
July 6 Venus in Gemini
August 2 Venus in Cancer
August 28 Venus in Leo
September 22 Venus in Virgo
October 16 Venus in Libra
November 9 Venus in Scorpio
December 3 Venus in Sagittarius
December 27 Venus in Capricorn

1986

January 20 Venus in Aquarius
February 13 Venus in Pisces
March 9 Venus in Aries
April 2 Venus in Taurus
April 26 Venus in Gemini
May 21 Venus in Cancer
June 15 Venus in Leo
July 11 Venus in Virgo
August 7 Venus in Libra
September 7 Venus in Scorpio

1987

January 7 Venus in Sagittarius
February 5 Venus in Capricorn
March 3 Venus in Aquarius
March 28 Venus in Pisces
April 22 Venus in Aries
May 17 Venus in Taurus
June 11 Venus in Gemini
July 5 Venus in Cancer
July 30 Venus in Leo
August 23 Venus in Virgo
September 16 Venus in Libra
October 10 Venus in Scorpio
November 3 Venus in Sagittarius
November 28 Venus in Capricorn
December 22 Venus in Aquarius

1988

January 15 Venus in Pisces
February 9 Venus in Aries
March 6 Venus in Taurus
April 3 Venus in Gemini
May 17 Venus in Cancer

May 27 Venus in Gemini
August 6 Venus in Cancer
September 7 Venus in Leo
October 4 Venus in Virgo
October 29 Venus in Libra
November 23 Venus in Scorpio
December 17 Venus in Sagittarius

1989

January 10 Venus in Capricorn
February 3 Venus in Aquarius
February 27 Venus in Pisces
March 23 Venus in Aries
April 16 Venus in Taurus
May 11 Venus in Gemini
June 4 Venus in Cancer
June 29 Venus in Leo
July 24 Venus in Virgo
August 18 Venus in Libra
September 12 Venus in Scorpio
October 8 Venus in Sagittarius
November 5 Venus in Capricorn
December 10 Venus in Aquarius

1990

January 16 Venus in Capricorn
March 3 Venus in Aquarius
April 6 Venus in Pisces
May 4 Venus in Aries
May 30 Venus in Taurus
June 25 Venus in Gemini
July 20 Venus in Cancer
August 13 Venus in Leo
September 7 Venus in Virgo
October 1 Venus in Libra

October 25 Venus in Scorpio
November 18 Venus in Sagittarius
December 12 Venus in Capricorn

1991

January 5 Venus in Aquarius
January 29 Venus in Pisces
February 22 Venus in Aries
March 18 Venus in Taurus
April 13 Venus in Gemini
May 9 Venus in Cancer
June 6 Venus in Leo
July 11 Venus in Virgo
August 21 Venus in Leo
October 6 Venus in Virgo
November 9 Venus in Libra
December 6 Venus in Scorpio
December 31 Venus in Sagittarius

1992

January 25 Venus in Capricorn
February 18 Venus in Aquarius
March 13 Venus in Pisces
April 7 Venus in Aries
May 1 Venus in Taurus
May 26 Venus in Gemini
June 19 Venus in Cancer
July 13 Venus in Leo
August 7 Venus in Virgo
August 31 Venus in Libra
September 25 Venus in Scorpio
October 19 Venus in Sagittarius
November 13 Venus in Capricorn
December 8 Venus in Aquarius

1993

January 3 Venus in Pisces
February 2 Venus in Aries
June 6 Venus in Taurus
July 6 Venus in Gemini
August 1 Venus in Cancer
August 27 Venus in Leo
September 21 Venus in Virgo
October 16 Venus in Libra
November 9 Venus in Scorpio
December 2 Venus in Sagittarius
December 26 Venus in Capricorn

1994

January 19 Venus in Aquarius
February 12 Venus in Pisces
March 8 Venus in Aries
April 1 Venus in Taurus
April 26 Venus in Gemini
May 21 Venus in Cancer
June 15 Venus in Leo
July 11 Venus in Virgo
August 7 Venus in Libra
September 7 Venus in Scorpio

1995

January 7 Venus in Sagittarius
February 4 Venus in Capricorn
March 2 Venus in Aquarius
March 28 Venus in Pisces
April 22 Venus in Aries
May 16 Venus in Taurus
June 10 Venus in Gemini
July 5 Venus in Cancer
July 29 Venus in Leo

August 23 Venus in Virgo
September 16 Venus in Libra
October 10 Venus in Scorpio
November 3 Venus in Sagittarius
November 27 Venus in Capricorn
December 21 Venus in Aquarius

1996

January 15 Venus in Pisces
February 9 Venus in Aries
March 6 Venus in Taurus
April 3 Venus in Gemini
August 7 Venus in Cancer
September 7 Venus in Leo
October 4 Venus in Virgo
October 29 Venus in Libra
November 23 Venus in Scorpio
December 17 Venus in Sagittarius

1997

January 10 Venus in Capricorn
February 3 Venus in Aquarius
February 27 Venus in Pisces
March 23 Venus in Aries
April 16 Venus in Taurus
May 10 Venus in Gemini
June 4 Venus in Cancer
June 28 Venus in Leo
July 23 Venus in Virgo
August 17 Venus in Libra
September 12 Venus in Scorpio
October 8 Venus in Sagittarius
November 5 Venus in Capricorn
December 12 Venus in Aquarius

1998

January 9 Venus in Capricorn
March 4 Venus in Aquarius
April 6 Venus in Pisces
May 3 Venus in Aries
May 29 Venus in Taurus
June 24 Venus in Gemini
July 19 Venus in Cancer
August 13 Venus in Leo
September 6 Venus in Virgo
September 30 Venus in Libra
October 24 Venus in Scorpio
November 17 Venus in Sagittarius
December 11 Venus in Capricorn

1999

January 4 Venus in Aquarius
January 28 Venus in Pisces
February 21 Venus in Aries
March 18 Venus in Taurus
April 12 Venus in Gemini
May 8 Venus in Cancer

June 5 Venus in Leo
July 12 Venus in Virgo
August 15 Venus in Leo
October 7 Venus in Virgo
November 9 Venus in Libra
December 5 Venus in Scorpio
December 31 Venus in Sagittarius

2000

January 24 Venus in Capricorn
February 18 Venus in Aquarius
March 13 Venus in Pisces
April 6 Venus in Aries
May 1 Venus in Taurus
May 25 Venus in Gemini
June 18 Venus in Cancer
July 13 Venus in Leo
August 6 Venus in Virgo
August 31 Venus in Libra
September 24 Venus in Scorpio
October 19 Venus in Sagittarius
November 13 Venus in Capricorn
December 8 Venus in Aquarius

HIS MARS

MARS IN ARIES

Get used to his snarling and growling. All of his aggressive energies are up-front—at least, you hope they are. If not, then he is a passive-aggressive Aries and that's far worse. Mars in Aries is a fighter, and often he begins fighting with the women he is most attracted to. He is completely baffled when they flee in tears and can't understand why another "good" relationship didn't work. It's best to deal with an Aries man as he stands—ready for conflict and action. Although he can sometimes appear polite and accommodating on the surface, this man really wants to love hard and rough. To stay happy, he requires physical toughness and a formidable opponent in his lovers.

Mars in Aries is not normally attracted to vulnerability in a woman, and sometimes he doesn't even like his women to be feminine in a passive way. Sex is a sport to him, in which wrestling and wriggling bodies provide the most fun. An athletic woman who knows her own mind, one who is regal and proud and not necessarily dainty, turns Mars in Aries on. Playing the shy, docile type will only invite him to be mean or combative and will inspire Mars in Aries to be cruel. Remember: Aries is mean because he wants you to stand up for yourself, to fight him strong and hard. Mars in Aries sees excessive kindness or forgiveness as a character flaw. So if you want a relationship with this man to last, remember to maintain your individuality, never act helpless, and prove to him that if given the chance, you could whip his butt easily, either through wit, brains, or brawn.

Yes, a love relationship with this man is complicated. He doesn't know where to put his aggressions. Make sure he never finds your weak spot, and make sure you figure out where his is. Then he'll stick around just to try to figure out how you beat him at his own game.

Most Compatible Venus Signs: Venus in Leo is the sultry goddess who puts the lead in this man's pencil; imagine now Mae West. Venus in Leo is the physical embodiment of female strength and she has the body to prove it. Venus in Leo, however, won't give in. Aries has to work. He always wants to be the master, but the roles have switched and Aries is the slave. Mars in Aries gets tired of being the strong one, and secretly, this is what he really wants—a strong woman who can take over, make the decisions, and do all the work. Another compatible sign is Venus in Sagittarius. She is free in body and spirit, and oftentimes athletic. Mars in Aries loves this in a woman: A warrior princess! Remember Jane Fonda's *Barbarella* movie character? This Sagittarian diva is Mars in Aries' dream woman. Think of *Barbarella* as you lead your Aries man around by that golden ring in his nose. After all, dears, this is what Mars in Aries *truly wants.*

Interesting Combos in Case You're Looking for Fireworks: Venus in Aquarius is just odd enough to keep Mars in Aries always guessing. Venus in Aquarius is not necessarily masculine (although she very well may be), but she shares traits with the masculine mind. She's interested in ideas more than feelings. As far as romance is concerned, well, she can take it with a grain of salt or kick it to the curb. That's because the Venus in Aquarius woman is probably the most balanced sign when it comes to Yin and Yang energies. She has both a man and a woman inside her. You never know which is going to come out. That's why she tends to like boys and girls pretty much the same. This is very titillating to Mars in Aries.

Venus Signs to Avoid Like the Plague: Venus in Pisces and Venus in Cancer feel like wet blankets to the Mars-in-Aries man; they suck up his energy and dampen his style. The clinging of these two signs is suffocating to a Mars in Aries, who loathes restrictions. In defense of his freedom, Aries will turn mean and ugly. Relationships between these signs take a great deal of patience, but being patient is simply not something for which Aries has the talent. If you still want this man, have an astrologer cast your charts and compare them. Perhaps the astrologer will find more favorable aspects by considering angles with the other planets. Sometimes positive aspects can override the negative factors between two horoscopes.

MARS IN TAURUS

This is one horny guy. Taurus is the sign of the voracious appetite and this includes his favorite areas of excess: money, food, and sex. After all, bullish Taurus is the sign of the senses, and, like his fixed-sign brother Leo, he wants to partake in all of the sweet banquets (or orgies) that life has to offer. There's the rub. Taurus is often a deeply conservative sign and wants to appear in control. He somewhat disapproves of his own urges but manages to justify them. The downside is that carnal pleasures still rule various aspects of his life.

On the other hand, Taurus can be judgmental, which only reveals how jealous he is of the sexual activities of others. This man likes sex to be comfortable and straight, but sometimes wants a threesome, because, after all, Taurus goes back for seconds and thirds. Like Scorpio, he just can't get enough of a good thing, whether it is sex partners, lucrative money deals, or desserts. He's a neck-kisser and for him, his neck and chest are highly erogenous zones. He may have a weakness for beauty pageant contestants. That's his sort of thing—frills, beauty, and status. Mars in Taurus men resemble generous and warm teddy bears, who like nothing better than a roll in the hay.

Although these men love sex and women even more than the average guy, Mars in Taurus is still traditional, opting for marriage and family rather than the promiscuous lifestyle of his youth. His sexual life (which can spin out of control and be quite excessive) is often curtailed by the hint of public approval or disapproval. In any event, he's a good guy, strong in the loins, a vigorous lover, but with warm hands and a warm heart. When committed to a long-term romance, Mars in Taurus may fantasize about your prettiest friends, yet he is loyal and seldom strays.

Most Compatible Venus Signs: Venus in Scorpio likes having sex as much as Mars in Taurus. This shared need for sensual pleasure is a strong and intimate bond that many marriages lack. There is often a conflict when it comes to frequency of sex in many marriages, but not so with this sexy combination. Although many astrology books would have you believe Mars in Taurus is also compatible with Venus in Capricorn, the latter can be a cold, calculating lover, interested more in money than sex. Those with Mars or Venus in Capricorn often have disappointing sex lives, or no sex life at all.

Interesting Combos in Case You're Looking for Fireworks: Venus in Leo is regal and proud and she loves beautiful objects the same way Taurus does. This Venus sign tends to be vain, however, while Mars in Taurus usually is not. This brings up the "slob factor." Although Taurus loves to buy, he is not very organized, either in his personal appearance or around his home. Venus in Leo cannot bear to see her initial romantic image of Taurus be shattered by his slacking off and general sloppiness. The sex is good between these two signs, but keep a mirror above the bed. Watching herself is Venus in Leo's main obsession and the mirror is Leo's favorite possession.

Venus Signs to Avoid Like the Plague: Venus in Gemini and Venus in Aquarius will dazzle in the bedroom, but they would likely give Mars in Taurus a coronary! After all, these signs tend to be flighty, flirtatious, and slightly disloyal. Taurus cannot tolerate disloyalty since he and Leo are the most loyal signs of all. He's not into surprises, and both Gemini and Aquarius lack the constancy Taurus looks for in a romance.

MARS IN GEMINI

More than a little friendly, this man has a roving eye and never stays in the same place for long. Flirtatious to the max, Mars in Gemini is the kind of guy who makes wives and girlfriends miserable. He doesn't inspire trust since he acts pretty much the same with all women: he flirts and teases, and likes nothing better than to woo them into bed. He's a sexual salesman, all right. Mars-in-Gemini men adore women and are always working on their next "conquest." Often, his philandering is unconscious. So he denies it and denies it, until the sex act occurs—"Whoops!" (he explains to his current mate) "I didn't mean to do that!" Often he is just as surprised as anyone is.

The Mars-in-Gemini man is attracted to intelligence in both sexes and doesn't find dummies particularly exciting, no matter how pretty they are. He likes smart women. In fact, he loves a brilliant woman, for she is the one he is meant to marry. His wife may occasionally have to worry about "bimbo eruptions," but other women who have little intellectual capacity will not hold his interest for long.

Loving a Mars-in-Gemini man can be a double-edged sword. He is vital and energetic. He is an adept, masterful lover. Mars in Gemini looks young and acts young. The bad part is, he sexually pursues the young. He's not perverted; he simply deludes himself into believing he's as young as they are. This can be a problem. (Middle age to a Gemini is around seventy-five.) To hold this man's interest, you must be current and up-to-date. You must also be a masterful kisser and a playful lover. But most of all, you must have a fluid mind and versatile interests to help him stay in one spot—next to you, of course.

Most Compatible Venus Signs: Mars in Gemini feels in harmony with the Venus in Libra woman. They share a love of words, sensual games and toys, and experimental sex. This couple may wish to invite a third party into their bedroom and have a threesome. After all, both are dual signs and have certain bisexual tendencies, and they are willing to explore this possibility in relationships. Mars in Gemini is also quite attracted to and compatible with Venus in Aquarius, even though she may seem like a girl from Planet X. Venus in Aquarius is full of quirky surprises. This will always keep Mars in Gemini coming back for more.

Interesting Combos in Case You're Looking for Fireworks: Mars in Gemini loves talk and this includes dirty talk. It may seem a little weird, possibly immature to the rest of us, but Venus in Scorpio is more than willing to supply it to keep her man happy. Venus in Scorpio is deeply passionate and sex is a vital aspect of her life. Anyone who wins this lady's love is a lucky lover. There are risks involved. Venus in Scorpio can be quite possessive and suspicious, while Mars in Gemini can be promiscuous and doesn't like the idea of being tied to one woman, especially a jealous one who gives him the third degree whenever he leaves the house.

Venus Signs to Avoid Like the Plague: Venus in Capricorn is rather stern and stoic. Plus, when it comes to sex, Venus in Capricorn freezes over whenever she's not in control and simply won't put out. Also, she isn't willing to give him some slack and can be highly critical. Mars in Gemini doesn't have time for these games.

MARS IN CANCER

This strong, sensitive guy holds his feelings in. When you first meet him, he will appear rather reserved and not at all moved by his own emotional needs. Cancer is one of those Water signs (Scorpio is the other one) who comes across as very firm and not particularly vulnerable. Mars in Cancer gives off this vibe: "Nothing can hurt me, not even you!" What you see is not a lack of emotion but self-protection. Mars in Cancer is sensitive to such an inordinate degree that he does not enter relationships too quickly or too easily. When he begins to fall in love, he can only remember past hurts. So Mars in Cancer worries, going over every angle of what could go wrong. He knows that if the relationship fails, he would be emotionally wiped out and it would be back to square one.

Sexually, this man is a wonderful lover, as he is eager to please the women in his life in many different ways. He has a soft, gentle quality when you get to know him, which is almost feminine but certainly not effeminate. He loves kissing breasts. The breasts and nipples are erogenous zones on him as well. The Mars-in-Cancer man remains strong and devoted as long as you can win his trust. The most intimate of signs, Mars in Cancer still shuns intimacy at first. Be kind to him, his daughters, sisters, or mother. Offer him empathy and reassurance, and he will remain the devoted friend and skillful lover he was born to be.

Most Compatible Venus Signs: The Water signs, Cancer, Scorpio, and Pisces, all share a certain type of telepathy. These signs are actually quite psychic on many levels, and naturally such an affinity for "vibes" and "what remains unsaid" will attract them to each other. Generally, their love affairs are long and lasting, and when they do end, there is still that emotional and psychic bond forever and always. Sexually speaking, Venus in Scorpio is an assertive and exciting lover for demure and insecure Mars in Cancer. Venus in Scorpio is not afraid to ask for or suggest unusual types of foreplay or positions. Cancer loves sex just as much as Scorpio but is shy about expressing his needs. Venus in Pisces is compatible as well. Both have huge imaginations that can spice up their sex life. Venus in Pisces is also psychically in tune with the deeper emotional needs of Mars in Cancer.

Interesting Combos in Case You're Looking for Fireworks: Venus in Leo should do the trick. As mentioned earlier, these two signs have a certain affinity for each other since one is the classic introvert and the other is the classic extrovert. Her flamboyant quality arouses desire in the conservative Mars-in-Cancer man. Normally, signs that are side-by-side are not necessarily compatible. The exception to this rule would be the signs of Cancer and Leo. Both signs are terribly romantic. Cancer is sentimental and private, while Leo is grandiose and seeks attention. Mars in Cancer is aroused by and proud of the attention Venus in Leo brings. Both signs are loyal and not in the least shallow. These are personalities who are moved by their passions, and their feelings always come first.

Venus Signs to Avoid Like the Plague: Venus in Aries moves too fast for Mars in Cancer. She is entirely too aggressive and wants to get physical faster than he does. Although there is a sexual tension between these signs, the basic incompatibility is too great for the relationship to really develop under the usual circumstances. Venus in Sagittarius is frank and honest, looking at life as a truth-or-dare game. This gets on the nerves of Mars in Cancer, who seeks safety and familiarity in his love life rather than a challenge.

MARS IN LEO

Although he is sometimes pompous and attention seeking, Mars in Leo is really not such a bad fellow. This man has great creative zeal. He's a mover and a shaker, and this includes in the bedroom. Sexually, Mars in Leo wants to be the center of the universe, making all of the important moves. At other times, he wants his lover on top so he can ease back, put his hands behind his head, and enjoy the show. Make him feel important during sex by telling him what a great lover he is. This noble sign is loyal but egotistical. In keeping with this, Mars in Leo can be a bit obnoxious when it comes to bragging about his accomplishments, not to mention when he reminds you what a great guy he is. In truth, he is worthy of admiration since he has big ideas and is able to bring them to reality.

Mars in Leo is quite charismatic. This man is never without a woman, and often two or three others on the side. He juggles them all with amazing intelligence and expertise. His lovemaking is focused and vigorous. He isn't afraid to tell you how beautiful you are. When having sex with a Mars in Leo man, make sure you moan and scream. This excites him incredibly. What is Mars in Leo's erogenous zone? Looking at his reflection in the mirror. Make sure you hang mirrors around your bed. After all, Mars in Leo adores making love to you, and himself, at the same time.

Most Compatible Venus Signs: Venus in Sagittarius requires plenty of exercise in order to chase her about. Many times, she can take men or leave them, and is more interested in the sport of love rather than settling down with just one guy. Usually, that's fine with Mars in Leo because a part of him feels the same way. Plus, he enjoys the athletics involved in making love to Venus in Sagittarius, who is blunt yet funny. Venus in Aries likes sex to be fast and rough, as if she is running a race, getting ready for her "peak experience" of having an orgasm with Mars in Leo, her true "marathon man."

Interesting Combos in Case You're Looking for Fireworks: Venus in Aquarius offers many surprises. Often she is a freaky, quirky artist-type. She grabs your attention by the very nature of her oddness (which is real, not put-on) and for being casually rebellious toward the status quo. Mars in Leo is unique, too, but he may not be so brave about it or allow it to show in public. Aquarius doesn't give a damn about what other people think, but Leo does. He wants to shine. Whenever Mars in Leo is with Venus in Aquarius, he is able to do both.

Venus Signs to Avoid Like the Plague: Venus in Virgo likes to conceal her love for sex and her tendency to be a bit promiscuous. She keeps many secrets from her bedroom, even though she appears shy and demure. Of course, she is. Mars in Leo doesn't go for the overcooked-oats type. Mars in Leo is drawn toward women who want attention almost as much as he does. So what about Venus in Capricorn? Forget it. This conservative winter sign freezes over Leo's summer sun.

Mars in Virgo

He thinks before he acts. Mars in Virgo builds a strategy in all matters and plays his love life like a game of chess. Despite the fact that his sign is called "virgin," he has great sensuality, and yet he is patient when it comes to sex. He can wait it out partly because he is a modest guy and is somewhat embarrassed or shy about sexual matters. He can be a bit of a puritan at times and at other times "sex-obsessed." He'd be as promiscuous as hell if he wasn't always glancing over his shoulder to see who was watching. Guilt over sexuality, which he learned from his parents, can make Mars in Virgo a bit jaded or warped. Therefore, he tends to be fond of strip clubs and other "fringe" sexual activity. Up front, he disapproves of promiscuity, all the while being attracted to it or practicing it. Women who wear their sexuality on their sleeves (and other places, too) entice him. To get sexual with this man too quickly, however, causes him to lose respect for you as well as for himself. Mars in Virgo is a serious guy. He wants to be sure he is right when he finally makes a commitment. Avoid sleaze and use a wholesome approach to your romantic and sexual life. Mars in Virgo must be able to give respect before he gives his love. Therefore, act respectable.

Most Compatible Venus Signs: The sensitivity of Mars in Virgo is most compatible with compassionate Venus in Pisces. These two signs, though opposite, share many things in common. Both signs are feeling-oriented, sensitive, and wound easily. To make the relationship work, however, Venus in Pisces must be willing to give up a few bad habits, many of which stem from not having a defined character or strong morals. Pisces is easily led, while Virgo stays strong. In this way, they complement each other. Venus in Taurus and Venus in Cancer are also good mates for Mars in Virgo.

Interesting Combos in Case You're Looking for Fireworks: Mars in Virgo is attracted to the willful, stirring spirit of Venus in

Sagittarius. She is as full of surprises as a grand jury testimony. Mars in Virgo and Venus in Sagittarius are fond of wide, open spaces. Both have a love of nature and a love of the nature of sex. You can't go wrong there. Venus in Gemini is funny, flirtatious, and talkative. She's a blast to be around when you first get to know her. Yet Mars in Virgo tends to be the strong, silent type, letting Venus in Gemini chatter away. This can eventually get on one's nerves, especially if one hates that sort of thing in the first place.

Venus Signs to Avoid Like the Plague: Arrogant Aries is not a sign that gets along well with vanishing Virgo. Both are steadfast in their approaches and are not likely to change. This creates conflicts, especially in the case of love affairs. A few off-the-cuff cutting remarks of Venus in Aries seem heartless and cruel to sensitive Mars in Virgo. Venus in Aquarius appears unemotional, lacking in sentimentality, and downright scary to Mars in Virgo, who always plays by the rules—unless he is riding his Harley, of course, but that's another matter entirely!

MARS IN LIBRA

Men and women alike love this man. Soft-spoken and charming to the max, Mars in Libra is the greatest seducer of all. Very few people have this much power to woo you, the ability to reassure you as if you are the only person in the world. When Mars in Libra seduces, he makes you feel it was all your idea. Does Bill Clinton ring a bell? Mars in Libra is a pleasant guy, that's for sure—but he can be manipulative and a moocher. Many Mars-in-Libra men choose mates who'll be the main breadwinner, women who will support them. Although Libra is a masculine cardinal sign, he understands what women need better than any other

Mars sign. He may be a philanderer, but he's not a cad. He doesn't ruthlessly use. He is actually quite fond of everyone with whom he has an affair. This doesn't mean Mars in Libra can't be monogamous. The majority of them are true to their lovers, but still, he can look. After all, Mars in Libra has a strong sense of beauty, and he likes his women to be very attractive—well, at least most of the time. At his worst, this man will string you along because he doesn't want to come to a decision of any kind. In reality, he can be rather dependent so he needs a strong partner who inspires a sense of authority. Is he worth it? Yes—yes!

Most Compatible Venus Signs: Venus in Aquarius should be his first choice. The love between John Lennon and Yoko Ono is a good example of the kind of intense bond created between the signs of Libra and Aquarius. Mars in Libra is rather dependent on his woman, while Venus in Aquarius is the one who isn't afraid to be different, the strong one who marches forward. (Well, at least her mate sees her as bold and strong.) These Air signs are buddies and pals with each other at first, but together, they form an awesome power. It's an affair of the heart and mind that shouldn't be taken lightly. Venus in Gemini also works well with Mars in Libra, because, let's face it, both are great kissers, and they share a love for words, puzzles, literature, and art. Venus in Gemini and Mars in Libra can have great sex just by using their hands and their mouths.

Interesting Combos in Case You're Looking for Fireworks: Mars in Libra considers Venus in Leo awesome, because after all, she is can be very, very beautiful. Venus in Leo is arresting to the eyes and senses. Mars in Libra picks out beautiful objects and mementos to give to Venus in Leo. Both have good taste and are materialistic so they are both working toward the same thing. When conversation gets boring, they can sit back and enjoy each other's good looks.

Venus Signs to Avoid Like the Plague: Venus in Scorpio can be rather controlling and is just no damned fun for Mars in Libra. He wants to gad about, as well as flirt with all of the attractive people he happens to meet—especially beautiful women. This drives envious Venus in Scorpio mad and an ugly scene normally ensues. Venus in Capricorn shares Mars in Libra's love of money and possessions. These signs, however, are basically incompatible, in the sense that Capricorn can outmanipulate a Libra anytime. Venus in Capricorn might be happy with the arrangement, but Mars in Libra would be miserable.

Mars in Scorpio

When you first see this man, he makes you want to purr—or growl! Mars in Scorpio has a strong effect on everyone. It's not that he's popular, but he is greatly admired. Nevertheless, many are afraid of him. Generally, no one is going to throw a surprise party for this man. They all fear him; he is that awesome. People sense that there is something deep and complicated to this man. Thus, they worry that he will use his power against them. He does have power: great charisma and great sexual power. Mars in Scorpio is the kind of man who inspires rumors of wild sex on the office copying machine and about the many notches in his belt. Here is the surprise: While Mars in Scorpio is definitely sexual (his sign rules the genitals), he is rarely promiscuous. Why? Like the other Water signs, the Mars-in-Scorpio man is shy and has trouble approaching the people he is most attracted to. Scorpio is one of the few signs who can be celibate for years, then swing back into a normal sex life as if he hadn't missed any of it at all. After all, Scorpio is the sign of extremes—it is either all or nothing. The lucky woman who gets this man will have many nights of bliss. The Mars-in-Scorpio man is a passionate, constant lover, but he isn't above using men and women just for sex. As a virtuoso of the erotic, this man not only gets under your skin, he works his way into your very soul. His love can be like a sugar high, like dope or another addiction. Don't be afraid to flaunt your own power around Mars in Scorpio. He dislikes weakness in people and respects only the powerful. If you play the doormat, you'll lose him. If you show him you're the Queen, he'll treat you like one.

Most Compatible Venus Signs: The other Water signs, Cancer and Pisces, have what Scorpio looks for in his lovers: depth and sensitivity. Scorpio is a sexual sign to be sure, with a sexual imagination and a high hormonal drive, but he is no alley cat. There must be a more compelling reason for a Scorpio to stick around, such as shared interests or similar emotional patterns.

Interesting Combos in Case You're Looking for Fireworks: Venus in Leo dazzles Mars in Scorpio, but she is apt to make him feel insecure and jealous. Venus in Leo has admirers and grabs attention, while Scorpio wants her all to himself. Still, the love-making can be dazzling between these two signs. A famous Leo, sex-goddess Mae West, once commented that Scorpios and Leos were the best lovers of the zodiac and she had tested them all. (As long as Scorpio didn't try to crowd her out of her mirror in the morning.) One can almost hear the titanic blonde bomb purr, "Ooh, Baby, Honey-man, why not come up and see me some time? It makes no difference to me what your sign is."

MARS IN SAGITTARIUS

If you want this man, consider growing an armor of thick skin.
He's frank and truthful, meaning he can also be very tactless. He
has lots of female friends, but you wouldn't necessarily call this
character "a ladies' man." He is well-liked, despite his brashness,
and honest to the point of being blunt. Women tend to pal
around with this guy. He's exciting, outspoken, and has a strong
point of view. It's doubtful he'd go to bat for you, even more
doubtful that he'd stand up and give you his chair—or give you
anything else, for that matter. He's just not chivalrous. He doesn't
even know the meaning of the word. A woman wishing to be
pampered would be greatly disappointed by this guy she once
found so dashing.

Mars in Sagittarius can be rugged, reckless, and attractive.
His devil-may-care attitude is somehow compelling; he just isn't
very sensitive. About the only time his passions rise is when he is
defending his opinions and, for certain, he has many to defend.
He is looking for a mate who is vivacious and a good dancer. Also,
keep in mind that this man can't stand clinging vines. Mars in
Sagittarius is certainly friendly, and he has a great deal of charm
to spread around the planet, but you can be assured that you're
not the only one he wants to bed or wed! After he does decide on
a mate, he wants her to be either his partner for adventure or a
partner in crime. He'll take you to hell in a handbasket and part
of the way back. Is he worth it? Yes. Yes! *Yes!* But in the end, only
you can decide.

Most Compatible Venus Signs: Venus in Aries can hold her
own against Mars in Sagittarius and this excites him. He is
drawn to women who are stronger than he is. He may even

admire athletic ability and physical strength, traits Aries is more than happy to provide. Neither sign is a strong admirer of sentiment. Venus in Leo is also a natural when it comes to loving a Mars-in-Sagittarius man. She's noble, beautiful, and has an aura of strength about her—all traits that Mars in Sagittarius secretly wishes he had.

Interesting Combos in Case You're Looking for Fireworks: The vivacious signs of Venus in Gemini and Venus in Aquarius attract the Mars-in-Sagittarius man. Both signs enjoy exploring and testing the limits as much as he does. The two Air signs, however, tend to push the envelope even more than Sagittarius does. He likes this.

Venus Signs to Avoid Like the Plague: The conservative Earth signs do not generally flow easily with Mars in Sagittarius. This, of course, includes sex. Mars in Sagittarius is very much into it, but only for a short amount of time. The Earth signs simmer for a long time before they smolder. These two types of energies are generally incompatible.

MARS IN CAPRICORN

The Mars-in-Capricorn man doesn't know where to put his emotions, so he puts them in a little box and keeps them there. This box is seldom out in the open and is almost never seen. Only when he is made to feel safe and secure is he able to open this box to show his love. In this respect the Mars-in-Capricorn man can be a bit mysterious, even wise and dignified. If the box is never opened, though, he comes across as cold. Lovers may claim that he is remote, and that they can never reach him. When a relationship breaks up with a Mars-in-Capricorn man, the woman often comes away feeling as if she never knew him at all—and, in reality, she probably didn't. This man thinks he has much to hide and believes he must maintain that "stiff upper lip."

There are other factors that contradict the mores of traditional romance. If you're a true romantic, you may not be overly impressed with this opportunistic guy once you get to know him. Often (although certainly not always) Mars in Capricorn will be more impressed with your bank account than with your charm or your good looks. After all, he is practical and is thinking about his own future. Thrifty and hard-working, the Mars-in-Capricorn man tends to be loyal and rarely every strays—unless he happens on a wealthy socialite with plenty of money to spend. Then the fairy-tale romance that you hoped for may have another ending.

This man is ambitious and wants to stay on top, in sex and every other aspect of his life. He may have had difficulty with a mother who was rather cold or controlling. He may have difficulties with women in general; however, Mars in Capricorn is charismatic. This looks-lucky sign gets even more handsome as he grows older. When Mars in Capricorn gives you special gifts, you'll know this man is serious. Just remember his "little box" and what it takes to make him feel safe.

Most Compatible Venus Signs: Venus in Virgo is a natural for Mars in Capricorn since she is demure and shares many of his practical values. Plus, Virgo reminds Mars in Capricorn when he needs to be more sensitive and aware of other people's feelings. Mars in Capricorn has a healthy sexual appetite, once it gets rolling. Venus in Taurus is the buxom, sensual mistress who can keep this guy happy in bed. Since he is not an overly sexual sign, it doesn't take a lot to keep this guy happy, but reaching him emotionally is entirely another matter.

Interesting Combos in Case You're Looking for Fireworks:
The Water signs soothe the emotional wounds that Mars in
Capricorn often carries with him. The patient and emotionally
deep Water signs of Cancer, Scorpio, and Pisces are also sexually
compatible. Venus in Cancer provides the best sex, while Venus in
Scorpio and Pisces provide imagination combined with passion, to
make this man's bedroom a far more interesting place.

Venus Signs to Avoid Like the Plague: What about Venus
in Aries with Mars in Capricorn? You don't put a billy goat in
the same pen with a ram, do you? At first, the two would
butt heads; if not separated, they would likely kill each other.
Therefore, a Venus-in-Aries woman coupled happily with a
Mars-in-Capricorn man would be quite the rarity. This doesn't
mean it can't happen. It just means *it shouldn't*. What about a
Venus-in-Leo woman? This golden cat wouldn't mind an occasional billy goat or two, but miserly Capricorn is not about to
spend the kind of money she is used to getting from her lovers
and friends.

MARS IN AQUARIUS

Keep in mind, he is more than unusual. This man is an *alien*.
Mars in Aquarius also has difficulties with women, because he
doesn't really understand them. He feels awkward around women,
especially the young ones, and is prone to having dry lips and
too many elbows and being all thumbs. Women puzzle him
greatly. Still, he sometimes wants to be one. Most of the time,
he'd prefer being the woman's friend, but face it, Mars in
Aquarius doesn't understand most men, either. This fellow is
more than a little odd. He's outrageously eccentric because he

wants to be. Mars in Aquarius makes his choices and doesn't care if he appears ridiculous. He calls the shots.

Romantically, what is the Mars-in-Aquarius man all about? He is looking for strangeness. He is into the varied and the unusual, including the sexually unusual. In fact, sex is the big issue with him—even more so than for a Scorpio. Often, Mars in Aquarius has unusual sexual peccadillos. He is attracted to women from a background different from the one in which he was raised. He looks for a lover who is out-of-the ordinary, such as women and men of different races. People of different ethnicities or religions fascinate him, and, of course, this carries over into romance. Artist-types, rebels, bohemians, or individuals involved in counterculture movements tend to be his "type." He is looking for women along the lines of Camille Paglia, k. d. lang, or Yoko Ono—atypically beautiful but androgynous. Without them, Mars in Aquarius might choose to be gay since bisexual fantasies and feelings are strong in this man. How can you keep him interested? Dare to be different. Learn to tease and shock. Continue to offer up a banquet of many sexual surprises.

Most Compatible Venus Signs: Venus in Gemini has the kind of androgynous appearance and aura that fascinates the Mars-in-Aquarius man. Plus, she is even more quick-witted than he is and certainly more funny. Venus in Libra is just as interested in ideas or art, especially that which is cutting-edge. Relationships between the Air signs tend to be lots of talking punctuated by brief yet intense love-making sessions. Truly beyond others, these are matches made on Venus and Mars!

Interesting Combos in Case You're Looking for Fireworks: Always the rebel at heart, equally rebellious Venus in Sagittarius can be quite the firecracker that Mars in Aquarius is searching for. With these two signs, however, don't expect much more than a friendship flavored with many delicious episodes of great sex.

Venus Signs to Avoid Like the Plague: Venus in Virgo has no trouble getting respect from Mars in Aquarius, but she is simply too old-fashioned for this up-and-coming guy. Venus in Cancer is stuck in the past, which bores Aquarius beyond tears, since his unique visions are in a future that many of us cannot yet imagine. Venus in Capricorn and Mars in Aquarius share the trait of appearing cold when it comes to love and sex. The most excitement this love duo could expect from a sexual romp would be to watch icicles form above their bed.

MARS IN PISCES

If you're looking for romance with an element of fun and fantasy, this is the man. Keep in mind, however, that Mars in Pisces is easily wounded, and despite the idealism he once believed in as a youth, he is now painfully jaded. At first this man comes across as sweet, vulnerable, and somewhat confused. He believes in the power of love but has so often been deflated, that there is a bit of a cynic in him, which pops out every once in a while. Does this sound like a contradiction? The very nature of Pisces the Fish is a contradiction—one fish swimming upstream and the other one going down. The main reason Mars in Pisces gets hurt is that he lacks the power to discriminate. For him, lovers often start out as acquaintances with "problems." The more they cry on his shoulder, the more his heartstrings begin to play. Pretty soon, he is immersed in the world of his lover's "woundedness," a scenario he relates to all too well. This man feels deeply. He is attuned to both people and his surroundings. He has a superb imagination. He is as intuitive and as sensitive as a woman. Put all of these traits together and you get hours and hours of incredible sex!

This man is no woman-hater; he prefers women. Yet there are a few rare Pisceans who eventually become hardened and even more cruel and brutal than the people who hurt them early in life. More than any other, Pisces is the sign of God, compassion, and peace. It is strange that more serial killers are born under the sign of Pisces than any other sign! The truth is, Pisces has few defenses. He rarely strikes back, but when he does, it can be in an extremely twisted way. Never fear. We know that *your* Pisces is one of the decent ones, but steer him away from drugs or any other kind of self-destructive, escapist behavior. On a more positive note, to attract this man, show some leg and adorn your feet with of a pair of sleek, gorgeous shoes—something elegant and metallic. (Pisceans are definitely into feet, you know.) Let him know that you love him in small but important ways. Mars in Pisces doesn't want much, just your love. If this one feels right to you, it would be wise to keep him around.

Most Compatible Venus Signs: Strong and sensitive Venus in Cancer often provides the most enduring love affair with Venus in Pisces. Plus, they are sexually quite compatible, preferring meaningful sex over lots of it. Mars in Pisces may have "different" kinds of interests similar to Mars in Aquarius; however, Pisces generally limits his interests to foot fetishes, role-playing, and, at times, masochistic elements in his lovemaking. After all, Mars in Pisces wants to be taken over by something "stronger than he is." Venus in Scorpio can provide this type of dominance and passion. Plus, she is not as likely to play "mommy" to Mars in Pisces as Venus in Cancer does. Venus in Taurus is also a good choice for the Pisces man, as long as she doesn't expect him to be the main breadwinner.

Interesting Combos in Case You're Looking for Fireworks:
Mars in Pisces wishes to be ruled or dominated. This makes Venus in Aries a natural draw for the Mars-in-Pisces man. He admires her strength and her dominance. She seems to know who she is, what she wants. He can wait on her hand and foot and play the passionate lover at times, there to do her bidding. Of course, Mars in Pisces loves being told what to do. It gives his life what he yearns for—structure. Although sex is often smoldering, these two Mars and Venus signs are generally not good for each other on a long-term basis. Often Mars in Pisces becomes miserable, hopeless, and hen-pecked, while Venus in Aries ends up disgusted and disappointed in her choice of men.

Venus Signs to Avoid Like the Plague: Although Venus in Sagittarius is a mutable sign like Mars in Pisces, as a couple they are a poor combination. Venus in Sagittarius could potentially lead Pisces down all of the wrong paths. While Venus in Sagittarius is merely an explorer and an observer who enjoys teetering around the edge of the volcano, Mars in Pisces tends to get pulled under by the lava tides. Any kind of wild partying, reckless sex, and destructive exploits may be little more than a diversion for a Sagittarius—but potentially dangerous for a Pisces. Venus in Gemini is as high-strung as Mars in Pisces is, but she is too blunt and unsympathetic about his constant commiserating.

If you cannot find you and your lover's Venus and Mars positions matching up with the previous descriptions, you might want to switch them around. For instance, look for *his* Venus sign and *her* Mars sign and read them accordingly. These planets are not so much about gender as they are about magnetism and attraction. Understanding the currents of sexual energy that are always present in our romantic relationships (and other ones as well) enables us to unlock the mysteries of sex and the most basic motivations between our lovers and ourselves. Pondering the wisdom behind this ancient art of astrology challenges us to let go of our judgments and to comprehend our lovers and our own sexual needs in a far deeper, more meaningful way.

MARS TABLES FROM 1935–2000

The following are astrological sign positions for the planet Mars from 1935 until 2000. Mars stays in a sign from as little as a few days to as long as twelve weeks. The dates listed below are the days when unruly Mars changed signs. Each date listed is when Mars enters an astrological sign. The date that follows is when the sign changes.

(PLEASE NOTE: When a planet seems to dip back into the previous sign, it is in what is called a "retrograde motion." This simply means that, from earth, Venus or Mars appears to have moved back into the previous sign for a few weeks. Simply look up your birth date and see in what sign it falls. Even if the planet is "retrograde" it is still in the sign described. Unless you are interested in learning advanced astrology, you needn't worry about retrogrades.)

1935
January 1 Mars in Libra
July 29 Mars in Scorpio
September 16 Mars in Sagittarius
October 28 Mars in Capricorn
December 7 Mars in Aquarius

April 1 Mars in Taurus
May 13 Mars in Gemini
June 25 Mars in Cancer
August 10 Mars in Leo
September 26 Mars in Virgo
November 14 Mars in Libra

1936
January 14 Mars in Pisces
February 22 Mars in Aries

1937
January 5 Mars in Scorpio
March 13 Mars in Sagittarius

May 14 Mars in Scorpio
August 8 Mars in Sagittarius
September 30 Mars in Capricorn
November 11 Mars in Aquarius
December 21 Mars in Pisces

1938
January 30 Mars in Aries
March 12 Mars in Taurus
April 23 Mars in Gemini
June 27 Mars in Cancer
July 22 Mars in Leo
September 7 Mars in Virgo
October 25 Mars in Libra
December 11 Mars in Scorpio

1939
January 29 Mars in Sagittarius
March 21 Mars in Capricorn
May 25 Mars in Aquarius
July 21 Mars in Capricorn
September 24 Mars in Aquarius
November 19 Mars in Pisces

1940
January 4 Mars in Aries
February 17 Mars in Taurus
April 1 Mars in Gemini
May 17 Mars in Cancer
July 3 Mars in Leo
August 19 Mars in Virgo
October 5 Mars in Libra
November 20 Mars in Scorpio

1941
January 4 Mars in Sagittarius
February 17 Mars in Capricorn
April 2 Mars in Aquarius
May 16 Mars in Pisces
July 2 Mars in Aries

1942
January 11 Mars in Taurus
March 7 Mars in Gemini
April 26 Mars in Cancer
June 14 Mars in Leo
August 1 Mars in Virgo
September 17 Mars in Libra
November 1 Mars in Scorpio
December 15 Mars in Sagittarius

1943
January 26 Mars in Capricorn
March 8 Mars in Aquarius
April 17 Mars in Pisces
May 27 Mars in Aries
July 7 Mars in Taurus
August 23 Mars in Gemini

1944
March 28 Mars in Cancer
May 22 Mars in Leo
July 12 Mars in Virgo
August 29 Mars in Libra
October 13 Mars in Scorpio
November 25 Mars in Sagittarius

1945
January 5 Mars in Capricorn

February 14 Mars in Aquarius
March 25 Mars in Pisces
May 2 Mars in Aries
June 11 Mars in Taurus
July 23 Mars in Gemini
September 7 Mars in Cancer
November 11 Mars in Leo
December 26 Mars in Cancer

1946

April 22 Mars in Leo
June 20 Mars in Virgo
August 9 Mars in Libra
September 24 Mars in Scorpio
November 6 Mars in Sagittarius
December 17 Mars in Capricorn

1947

January 25 Mars in Aquarius
March 4 Mars in Pisces
April 11 Mars in Aries
May 21 Mars in Taurus
July 1 Mars in Gemini
August 13 Mars in Cancer
October 1 Mars in Leo
December 1 Mars in Virgo

1948

February 12 Mars in Leo
May 18 Mars in Virgo
July 17 Mars in Libra
September 3 Mars in Scorpio
October 17 Mars in Sagittarius
November 26 Mars in Capricorn

1949

January 4 Mars in Aquarius
February 11 Mars in Pisces
March 21 Mars in Aries
April 30 Mars in Taurus
June 10 Mars in Gemini
July 23 Mars in Cancer
September 7 Mars in Leo
October 27 Mars in Virgo
December 26 Mars in Libra

1950

March 28 Mars in Virgo
June 11 Mars in Libra
August 10 Mars in Scorpio
September 25 Mars in Sagittarius
November 6 Mars in Capricorn
December 15 Mars in Aquarius

1951

January 22 Mars in Pisces
March 1 Mars in Aries
April 10 Mars in Taurus
May 21 Mars in Gemini
July 3 Mars in Cancer
August 18 Mars in Leo
October 5 Mars in Virgo
November 24 Mars in Libra

1952

January 20 Mars in Scorpio
August 27 Mars in Sagittarius
October 12 Mars in Capricorn
November 21 Mars in Aquarius

December 30 Mars in Pisces

1953
February 8 Mars in Aries
March 20 Mars in Taurus
May 1 Mars in Gemini
June 14 Mars in Cancer
July 29 Mars in Leo
September 14 Mars in Virgo
November 1 Mars in Libra
December 20 Mars in Scorpio

1954
February 9 Mars in Sagittarius
April 12 Mars in Capricorn
July 3 Mars in Sagittarius
August 24 Mars in Capricorn
October 21 Mars in Aquarius
December 4 Mars in Pisces

1955
January 15 Mars in Aries
February 26 Mars in Taurus
April 19 Mars in Gemini
May 26 Mars in Cancer
July 11 Mars in Leo
August 27 Mars in Virgo
October 13 Mars in Libra
November 29 Mars in Scorpio

1956
January 14 Mars in Sagittarius
February 28 Mars in Capricorn
April 14 Mars in Aquarius

June 3 Mars in Pisces
December 6 Mars in Aries

1957
January 28 Mars in Taurus
March 17 Mars in Gemini
May 4 Mars in Cancer
June 21 Mars in Leo
August 8 Mars in Virgo
September 24 Mars in Libra
November 8 Mars in Scorpio
December 23 Mars in Sagittarius

1958
February 3 Mars in Capricorn
March 17 Mars in Aquarius
April 27 Mars in Pisces
June 7 Mars in Aries
July 21 Mars in Taurus
September 21 Mars in Gemini
October 29 Mars in Taurus

1959
February 10 Mars in Gemini
April 10 Mars in Cancer
June 1 Mars in Leo
July 20 Mars in Virgo
September 5 Mars in Libra
October 21 Mars in Scorpio
December 3 Mars in Sagittarius

1960
January 14 Mars in Capricorn
February 23 Mars in Aquarius

April 2 Mars in Pisces
May 11 Mars in Aries
June 20 Mars in Taurus
August 2 Mars in Gemini
September 21 Mars in Cancer

1961

February 5 Mars in Gemini
February 7 Mars in Cancer
May 6 Mars in Leo
June 28 Mars in Virgo
August 17 Mars in Libra
October 1 Mars in Scorpio
November 13 Mars in Sagittarius
December 24 Mars in Capricorn

1962

February 1 Mars in Aquarius
March 12 Mars in Pisces
April 19 Mars in Aries
May 28 Mars in Taurus
July 9 Mars in Gemini
August 22 Mars in Cancer
October 11 Mars in Leo

1963

June 3 Mars in Virgo
July 27 Mars in Libra
September 12 Mars in Scorpio
October 25 Mars in Sagittarius
December 5 Mars in Capricorn

1964

January 13 Mars in Aquarius

February 20 Mars in Pisces
March 29 Mars in Aries
May 7 Mars in Taurus
June 17 Mars in Gemini
July 30 Mars in Cancer
September 15 Mars in Leo
November 6 Mars in Virgo

1965

June 29 Mars in Libra
August 20 Mars in Scorpio
October 4 Mars in Sagittarius
November 14 Mars in Capricorn
December 23 Mars in Aquarius

1966

January 30 Mars in Pisces
March 9 Mars in Aries
April 17 Mars in Taurus
May 28 Mars in Gemini
July 11 Mars in Cancer
August 25 Mars in Leo
October 12 Mars in Virgo
December 4 Mars in Libra

1967

February 12 Mars in Scorpio
March 31 Mars in Libra
July 19 Mars in Scorpio
September 10 Mars in Sagittarius
October 23 Mars in Capricorn
December 1 Mars in Aquarius

1968

January 9 Mars in Pisces

February 17 Mars in Aries
March 27 Mars in Taurus
May 8 Mars in Gemini
June 21 Mars in Cancer
August 5 Mars in Leo
September 21 Mars in Virgo
November 9 Mars in Libra
December 29 Mars in Scorpio

1969

February 25 Mars in Sagittarius
September 21 Mars in Capricorn
November 4 Mars in Aquarius
December 15 Mars in Pisces

1970

January 24 Mars in Aries
March 7 Mars in Taurus
April 18 Mars in Gemini
June 2 Mars in Cancer
July 18 Mars in Leo
September 3 Mars in Virgo
October 20 Mars in Libra
December 6 Mars in Scorpio

1971

January 23 Mars in Sagittarius
March 12 Mars in Capricorn
May 3 Mars in Aquarius
November 6 Mars in Pisces
December 26 Mars in Aries

1972

February 10 Mars in Taurus

March 27 Mars in Gemini
May 12 Mars in Cancer
June 28 Mars in Leo
August 15 Mars in Virgo
September 30 Mars in Libra
November 15 Mars in Scorpio
December 30 Mars in Sagittarius

1973

February 12 Mars in Capricorn
March 26 Mars in Aquarius
May 8 Mars in Pisces
June 20 Mars in Aries
August 12 Mars in Taurus
October 29 Mars in Aries
December 24 Mars in Taurus

1974

February 27 Mars in Gemini
April 20 Mars in Cancer
June 9 Mars in Leo
July 27 Mars in Virgo
September 12 Mars in Libra
October 28 Mars in Scorpio
December 10 Mars in Sagittarius

1975

January 21 Mars in Capricorn
March 3 Mars in Aquarius
April 11 Mars in Pisces
May 21 Mars in Aries
July 1 Mars in Taurus
August 14 Mars in Gemini
October 17 Mars in Cancer
November 25 Mars in Gemini

1976
March 18 Mars in Cancer
May 16 Mars in Leo
July 6 Mars in Virgo
August 24 Mars in Libra
October 8 Mars in Scorpio
November 20 Mars in Sagittarius

1977
January 1 Mars in Capricorn
February 9 Mars in Aquarius
March 20 Mars in Pisces
April 27 Mars in Aries
June 6 Mars in Taurus
July 17 Mars in Gemini
September 1 Mars in Cancer
October 26 Mars in Leo

1978
January 26 Mars in Cancer
April 10 Mars in Leo
June 14 Mars in Virgo
August 4 Mars in Libra
September 19 Mars in Scorpio
November 2 Mars in Sagittarius
December 12 Mars in Capricorn

1979
January 20 Mars in Aquarius
February 27 Mars in Pisces
April 7 Mars in Aries
May 16 Mars in Taurus
June 26 Mars in Gemini
August 8 Mars in Cancer

September 24 Mars in Leo
November 19 Mars in Virgo

1980
March 11 Mars in Leo
May 4 Mars in Virgo
July 10 Mars in Libra
August 29 Mars in Scorpio
October 12 Mars in Sagittarius
November 22 Mars in Capricorn
December 30 Mars in Aquarius

1981
February 6 Mars in Pisces
March 17 Mars in Aries
April 25 Mars in Taurus
June 5 Mars in Gemini
July 18 Mars in Cancer
September 2 Mars in Leo
October 21 Mars in Virgo
December 16 Mars in Libra

1982
August 3 Mars in Scorpio
September 20 Mars in Sagittarius
October 31 Mars in Capricorn
December 10 Mars in Aquarius

1983
January 17 Mars in Pisces
February 25 Mars in Aries
April 5 Mars in Taurus
May 16 Mars in Gemini
June 29 Mars in Cancer

August 13 Mars in Leo
September 30 Mars in Virgo
November 18 Mars in Libra

1984
January 11 Mars in Scorpio
August 17 Mars in Sagittarius
October 5 Mars in Capricorn
November 15 Mars in Aquarius
December 25 Mars in Pisces

1985
February 2 Mars in Aries
March 15 Mars in Taurus
April 26 Mars in Gemini
June 9 Mars in Cancer
July 25 Mars in Leo
September 10 Mars in Virgo
October 27 Mars in Libra
December 14 Mars in Scorpio

1986
February 2 Mars in Sagittarius
March 28 Mars in Capricorn
October 9 Mars in Aquarius
November 26 Mars in Pisces

1987
January 8 Mars in Aries
February 20 Mars in Taurus
April 5 Mars in Gemini
May 21 Mars in Cancer
July 6 Mars in Leo
August 22 Mars in Virgo

October 8 Mars in Libra
November 24 Mars in Scorpio

1988
January 8 Mars in Sagittarius
February 22 Mars in Capricorn
April 6 Mars in Aquarius
May 22 Mars in Pisces
July 13 Mars in Aries
October 23 Mars in Pisces
November 1 Mars in Aries

1989
January 19 Mars in Taurus
March 11 Mars in Gemini
April 29 Mars in Cancer
June 16 Mars in Leo
August 3 Mars in Virgo
September 19 Mars in Libra
November 4 Mars in Scorpio
December 18 Mars in Sagittarius

1990
January 29 Mars in Capricorn
March 11 Mars in Aquarius
April 20 Mars in Pisces
May 31 Mars in Aries
July 12 Mars in Taurus
August 31 Mars in Gemini
December 14 Mars in Taurus

1991
January 21 Mars in Gemini
April 3 Mars in Cancer

May 26 Mars in Leo
July 15 Mars in Virgo
September 1 Mars in Libra
October 16 Mars in Scorpio
November 29 Mars in Sagittarius

May 25 Mars in Virgo
July 21 Mars in Libra
September 7 Mars in Scorpio
October 20 Mars in Sagittarius
November 30 Mars in Capricorn

1992
January 9 Mars in Capricorn
February 18 Mars in Aquarius
March 28 Mars in Pisces
May 5 Mars in Aries
June 14 Mars in Taurus
July 26 Mars in Gemini
September 12 Mars in Cancer

1996
January 8 Mars in Aquarius
February 15 Mars in Pisces
March 24 Mars in Aries
May 2 Mars in Taurus
June 12 Mars in Gemini
July 25 Mars in Cancer
September 9 Mars in Leo
October 30 Mars in Virgo

1993
April 27 Mars in Leo
June 23 Mars in Virgo
August 12 Mars in Libra
September 27 Mars in Scorpio
November 9 Mars in Sagittarius
December 20 Mars in Capricorn

1997
January 3 Mars in Libra
March 8 Mars in Virgo
June 19 Mars in Libra
August 14 Mars in Scorpio
September 28 Mars in Sagittarius
November 9 Mars in Capricorn
December 18 Mars in Aquarius

1994
January 28 Mars in Aquarius
March 7 Mars in Pisces
April 14 Mars in Aries
May 23 Mars in Taurus
July 3 Mars in Gemini
August 16 Mars in Cancer
October 4 Mars in Leo
December 12 Mars in Virgo

1998
January 25 Mars in Pisces
March 4 Mars in Aries
April 13 Mars in Taurus
May 24 Mars in Gemini
July 6 Mars in Cancer
August 20 Mars in Leo
October 7 Mars in Virgo
November 27 Mars in Libra

1995
January 22 Mars in Leo

1999
January 26 Mars in Scorpio
May 5 Mars in Libra
July 5 Mars in Scorpio
September 2 Mars in Sagittarius
October 17 Mars in Capricorn
November 26 Mars in Aquarius

2000
January 4 Mars in Pisces

February 12 Mars in Aries
March 23 Mars in Taurus
May 3 Mars in Gemini
June 16 Mars in Cancer
August 1 Mars in Leo
September 17 Mars in Virgo
November 4 Mars in Libra
December 23 Mars in Scorpio

FOUR

BUYING THE PERFECT GIFT FOR THE PERFECT MATE

One of the most fascinating elements of astrology and the Sun sign is that they affect our deepest motivations and govern whom we choose to love and find attractive. Another amazing thing about our horoscopes and Sun signs is that not only do they influence the way we appear to others, our signs affect our tastes and our interests, as well as the subjects we go back to time and again. Although Sun signs are only one part of the horoscope, their influence is seen and felt in the choices we make.

You would be hard pressed to find an individual born under the sign of Cancer who isn't somehow fascinated by history—this might be family history, world history, or tribal history. At the same time, an individual born under Aquarius would not be very interested. Typically, Aquarians view the past as tired, dull, and finished. Only the tantalizing possibilities of the future fascinate Aquarius, who is much more in tune with future trends than history.

In various ways, our horoscopes, and most specifically our astrological signs, have influence over what we will like and dislike. After all, the signs we are born under color our view of life. The signs and stars affect our consciousness both within and without. It is only natural our astrological signs would also determine our interests and attractions.

We know that certain signs have a more conventional approach or attitude when it comes to areas of interest, whereas other signs thrive on the new and different. Yet even within those parameters, there are distinct differences. For instance, the signs Cancer and Capricorn are rather reserved in their individual tastes; however, Capricorn is pragmatic whereas Cancer is romantic. That can be a big difference when selecting the perfect gift for your lover.

Understanding your mate's personal style is crucial in gift giving. Giving the perfect gift shows that you love and understand your mate in a way that others do not. Gift giving can help bond the casual relationship and transform it into something far more intimate and lasting.

Do you know what your lover likes?

Read on to understand the inner life, the personal tastes as well as the preferences, the likes and dislikes of the following astrological signs. Once you understand the workings of your own natal sign, you will also understand the tastes and perhaps even the eccentricities of your lover's sign. Your gift giving will be more successful and there will be fewer unhappy surprises.

ARIES

Think *passion*—but without the mystery of a Scorpio. Aries is all revved up and ready to go—no surprises there! If you're confused over what to buy your Aries, just make sure it is *red*. A dozen red roses, a ruby ring, or an art piece representing a crimson sunset are ideal choices. Games that challenge mentally and physically are always a hit for this Mars-ruled sign. Sports items, for males and females alike, can't go wrong because the Ram thrives on competition. Spicy Indian and Mexican foods are the perfect birthday meal for Aries, topped off with cinnamon ice cream. Buying Aries a football, a tennis racquet, a barbecue, or expensive candles in shades of scarlet are perfect ways to show your love. After all, Aries loves to play with fire! Self-help books on how to "win" and "achieve" or books about famous wars are certain to interest an Aries. Exercise equipment and workout clothes appeal to Aries individuals, as they emphasize the need to win and to come out on top. Birthday cards that point out Aries is "Number 1" are a sure way of stirring the fires of Aries' love.

You might consider a biography of master magician and fellow-Aries Harry Houdini. Your Aries would also be interested in books on magic tricks or on how to overcome their foes. Aries people tend to go for things that are sleek, fast, and red with noisy motors—a little red sports car, perhaps? (Maybe you can allow Aries to borrow yours.) Trips out West, to places like the Grand Canyon, give Aries people plenty of room to move around. Since Aries has frequent headaches, a soothing eye mask, a sensual massage, or a bottle of the herb feverfew is sure to be appreciated by this head-banging sign. As far as "gift" foods are concerned, buy Aries some blood oranges, pomegranates, chili peppers, cinnamon candies, or a bottle of tequila. After all, like sex, Aries wants things *hot*. So when you wrap your gift, make sure there's a big, red bow on top!

TAURUS

This depends on what type of Taurus you are dating. Taurus is either artistic and refined or earthy to the point of being vulgar. The earthy type of Taurus enjoys objects or gifts that are either practical or rustic in nature. This sign generally goes for things that are natural to the point of being rough: anything made from trees with knots and rings, or stones with bumps still intact. If you choose cologne for your Taurus, then the scent should be something with a "woodsy" smell, like the aroma of cedar or spring grass.

For clothing, pick something in rich browns with just a hint of red and woodsy green, like the color of pine needles on clay earth leading deep into the forest. These are the essential colors that Taurus adores. A fancy leather wallet or an informative guide on how to start your own business and make lots of money appeals to Taureans of all kinds. Sticking a book of stamps or a gift certificate to an outlet store in with your card will thrill this miserly Bull. Taurus loves nothing more than saving money.

The more romantic, refined Taurus appreciates tickets to the ballet or a concert of classical music. Musical instruments, such as a piccolo or flute with music lessons, all make great gifts for Taurus people since this gentle Bull is the most musical sign of all. Singing lessons would also be the kind of luxury Taurus would not usually indulge in. Music boxes with lots of gold and ivory colors and classical scenes are the ideal gift for Taureans of either sex.

Venus-ruled Taurus loves art. A print of one of the surrealistic paintings of fellow-Taurus Salvador Dali would certainly please the more sophisticated Bull; however, if you suspect that your Taurus has never even heard of Salvador Dali, a miniature oil painting of a pastoral scene with lots of green and grazing animals would surely be a hit. Taurus loves nature even more than he loves art.

For Taurus women, choose a choker necklace with crystals, lots of sparkle, and matching earrings. Buy Taurus a state-of-the-art CD player, or the latest CD by Barbra Streisand or Pearl Jam. A dream vacation for Taurus would be going to Las Vegas and striking it rich. The most romantic gift would be to buy a tree for the two of you to plant together. So make sure your tree has a nice aroma and is very strong—just like your Taurus!

GEMINI

Consider a high-tech telephone with all kinds of buttons and features, or an answering machine with unlimited uses. Books of any kind appeal to Gemini, but the Twins are usually most fond of nonfiction, information-packed books. (Gemini seldom has patience for novels.) So sneak a peek at Gemini's personal library to find out the best topics to choose. Did you find only magazines? So typical of Gemini. Go buy your Gemini subscriptions to the most expensive and hip magazines around. Just make sure the magazines are chock-full of facts, just like Gemini's brain. Also, make sure the books have information not readily available to the general public; Gemini loves being the know-it-all.

Books on how to write, publish, or make a speech are forever inspiring to a Gemini. After all, they cherish words. You can tell this by the way Geminis talk endlessly. Geminis also gesture with their hands a lot, so gloves make an excellent present in fall and winter. Fill crazy, colorful boxes with all kinds of fun knick-knacks and surprises. Include a birthday card with a dirty joke and you won't go wrong. Geminis can be very tawdry. No sign appreciates surprises as much as a Gemini and this includes a huge, smashing, surprise birthday party with lots of confetti. Plan to have your Gemini's party in an unusual place such as an amusement park or a restaurant with a childhood theme since Gemini is the biggest kid of all. Include lots of balloons in rainbow colors and a gag gift. It's next to impossible to embarrass a Gemini; most of them have no shame.

People born under the sign of the Twins are in love with shiny things. A blue topaz ring with an unusual cut or a crazy pair of sunglasses with reflective glass are bound to appeal to them. Those under the influence of this chatty Air sign also tend to like windbreakers, raincoats, and umbrellas. After all, Gemini is both the sign of wind and hot Air. Trivia games appeal to your average Gemini—especially those that can be played on the computer. Twins love testing their wit against the intelligence of others. They almost always win. Also, consider buying Gemini wind chimes—the perfect gift! Wind chimes remind Gemini to be quiet and just listen. It helps him focus on his own thoughts, feelings, and views.

Scandalous biographies make good presents since they involve elements of what pleases Gemini most—gossip! Books on audio make great gifts for the Twins. Geminis tend to pretend they read a lot, when in reality they have little patience or desire to get through a weighty book. The twins do like to write, however, and they write very well, so buy your Gemini a fancy journal book. Expensive writing utensils, headphones, and cutting-edge technology are excellent gift choices. Drawing lessons, flying lessons, and drum lessons are sure to appeal. Gemini is also fond of the colors yellow, orange, and green. With Gemini in mind, just think uniqueness and versatility.

CANCER

The most personal connection for Cancer is a connection to the past so start browsing the antique stores first. Make Cancer's gift romantic or at least silver. Consider items with images of the planets, stars, and moon—soft, misty, and evocative! Victorian shadow boxes filled with seashells, books on history or on the paintings of Frida Kahlo, or a book or software on how to research the family tree are sure to delight a Cancer. Make sure that the gift you give your Cancerian has an aged or antique appearance. Satin pillowcases, bed sheets, a gorgeous pair of silk pajamas (the color of moonlight, of course!), or a dream journal are perfect gifts for this most imaginative dreamer in the zodiac. A gourmet meal over candlelight and a fantasy-driven gothic novel will make Cancer want to curl up in your arms and dream the night away. Stories, movies, or games involving mysteries and unsolved crimes tend to fascinate those born under the sign of the Cancer. Moonchildren are highly mysterious and are also attracted to globes, nesting eggs, and pearls.

Other perfect gifts for this early summer sign might be a set of silverware. (Cancers are as wild about silver as they are about moonlight!) Other great presents are a cookbook of favorite recipes, a book of family photos or pictures capturing your happiest times, or a trip out of town to someplace quaint that is both historic and romantic. A handsomely framed print of Cancer's family crest is absolutely ideal. Whether merited or not, Cancer is proud of his family heritage and his connection to history. So the best place for Cancer's birthday party would be around the family table with his most intimate and also childhood friends present.

Guides and books on how to build or decorate houses appeal to Cancer. To Cancer, the home is the kingdom. So when buying furnishings, Cancer is fond of floral rugs, overstuffed chairs, and anything that appeals to those who love elegance. The furnishings must also be comfortable. This ultrasensitive sign dreams and pines after the perfect abode.

Moonchildren greatly appreciate handcrafted objects. Therefore, other great gifts might be an adorable beaded lampshade or a vest that you decorate with Cancer's favorite buttons, patches, or pins. Those born under the sign of Cancer tend to be drawn to items related to early America or the Civil War. This would include documentaries, books, sepia-toned postcards, lithographs, or just about anything that evokes a sense of the past. Mysteries and books on how to develop psychic ability, or creative writing and art classes, make ideal gifts for this richly imaginative sign. Although Cancer is probably the greatest helper and caretaker in the zodiac, deep in his soul Cancer knows he is *really* an artist.

Leo

Look for the most elaborate mirror you can find. Wrap the whole thing in gold paper and tie on a big gold bow. On the card write, "I brought you something that *I* adore! Look inside the glass and see what it is!" As one who thrives on adulation, Leo will be thrilled. Such a card and gift is the most romantic message you could ever give this Lion-hearted sign. It is very important for Leo to feel that he measures up to others. He must not only be *equal*, but a cut above the rest to really feel secure. Hence, Leo is always checking himself in the mirror.

Another item that is sure to please Leo is to find a favorite photo and have his portrait painted or sketched from it by a professional artist. Put Leo's portrait in an elaborate, gilded frame and Leo should be quite pleased—as long as the portrait is flattering. If you feel the relationship is starting to move into a more serious area, you can also include yourself in the picture.

When considering other gifts, remember that most Leos prefer items that are loud and attention-grabbing. Some astrologers believe that Leo has the worst taste of all the signs. I think that Leos are either "off-the-mark" when it comes to fashion, or their sense of style is absolutely impeccable. Keep in mind that favorite colors for Leo are gold, citrus green, bright red, and burnt orange. Leo is ruled by the Sun and thus is generally open and optimistic. Things that are dark and foreboding, in general, would not appeal to this summer Lion. In keeping with this, buy Leo a jacket that evokes a sense of the military dressed in its finest. Leo loves badges, pins, and tokens of honor. Clothing with animal prints appeals equally to male and female Leos. A flowing scarf that can be tossed over the shoulder or worn knotted around the throat is the ideal accessory for the Lion-hearted. When you think of Leo, think *dramatic*.

Leo prefers books on how to become rich and famous (although most Leos prefer fame over money), books on fabulously well-known people and their dynasties, and books about British royalty of any day or age. Also fascinating to Leo are the cultures of Africa and ancient Egypt. So any gifts that reflect these interests are bound to please Leo. In terms of jewelry, just make sure it's weighty and real gold. Stationery with Leo's name embossed on it is sure to impress his friends, and this is what Leo truly loves—*attention!*

To honor your Leo love, you can throw a party in a public place just so Leo can bask in the fact that all eyes are on him. Be sure to videotape the proceedings. Make a big production out of the whole deal. Be sure there are many gifts. Leo doesn't care if the gifts are expensive or not; Leo just wants to be certain that everyone loves him! A camera is a vital thing for a Leo to have, so you might consider surprising Leo with an upgraded VCR. If you want Leo all to yourself during your special celebration, though, a toast of champagne to each other in front of a fireplace or bonfire is the ideal place to capture Leo's big heart.

VIRGO

Some of Virgo's favorite things are fancy organizers, expensive-looking briefcases, and calculators. When buying Virgo an item of clothing, make sure it is the exact color of cocoa wheats! Virgo loves anything to be in the natural colors of light brown and especially taupe. Lovely earth-toned baskets filled with soaps (oatmeal, sandalwood, honey, and almonds are favorite fragrances), healing herbs, expensive nuts, and aromatic oils are sure to please Virgo. Also, books about home remedies or the meaning and healing attributes of herbs are sure to fascinate Virgo.

A good place to start searching for Virgo's gift is in your neighborhood health food store. They usually sell the kinds of soaps and oils that Virgo loves—all natural. An already-paid-for visit to an acupuncturist, massage therapist, or chiropractor will delight health-conscious Virgo more than you know.

A file cabinet made of plain wood, a word processor, a free dry-cleaning, and trivia games based on numbers, words, or TV shows are all sure to please Virgo. Buy this sign of the Virginal Maiden a loom, a broom, a marionette, a set of antique books, or books about witchcraft. I know, strange, isn't it?

Conservative Virgo is oddly attracted to the themes of witchcraft, but most especially to nature-based Wicca, the religion of witches. Part of this stems from Virgo being an Earth sign, but also from Virgo's definite wild streak, which is not always apparent. This wild streak comes out in very surprising ways, however—even for a Virgo!

All in all, though, Virgo remains sensible. Therefore, when picking out a gift for Virgo, whatever gift you buy must always have a practical angle—a pretty but functional hat, durable shoes, and a conservative shirt that pretty much looks the same as his other shirts. Usually you can spot a Virgo pretty quickly. Virgo is always wearing the same uniform: tan pants, blue shirt, brown belt, and brown loafers. When going for something different for Virgo, make sure the gift remains *understated*. Unlike Leo, Virgo doesn't want attention. Virgo feels that if he attracts attention, he will also attract criticism and criticism is something Virgo dreads.

Other excellent gift choices for Virgo might include a Book of Days, framed prints of unicorns, art instruction books that emphasize drawing techniques, a garment bag, loungewear, crystals and gemstones, puzzles, or a laptop computer. A shopping outing to *used* bookstores, coffee shops, and places that sell great stuff real cheap puts your practical Virgo in seventh heaven. Top this off with an escape to an elegant bed and breakfast inn, with the promise that Virgo won't "worry" for an entire day!

LIBRA

Go to a department store and pick out the most gorgeous or lavish thing that you can afford. Make sure your prize is wrapped up nicely with matching tags, ribbons, and bows. Make sure everything smells nice and looks grand. Pay attention to all the frills. Venus-ruled Libra goes for beauty first, and, unlike Virgo, the gift does not have to be functional. Libra is one sign that loves to collect dolls, models of anything, and all types of fascinating knick-knacks. In other words, Librans go for fascinating, gratuitous junk.

In fact, Librans are more apt to go for things that speak to their need for extreme luxury rather than anything practical. Get Libra something useful, like a set of dishes or towels, and this sign will end up rather insulted. Therefore, when shopping for Libra, look for designer clothing, miniature oil paintings, sinful desserts, fancy candies, silk clothing, and various kinds of oils and potions that keeps Libra's skin looking and smelling nice. Libra loves perfume and cologne in designer bottles—but don't be cheap with imitations. Libra is a classy sign. Those born under the sign of the Scales are also fond of art but mostly the traditional kind that emphasizes beauty over meaning.

Another ideal place to start looking for Libra's present would be a museum gift shop, which has many classy and unusual items. Even an inexpensive gift, like a packet of art postcards, is bound to delight Libra. Other winners for Libra might be a grooming kit, a make-up mirror, expensive cosmetics, a romantic figurine, angel statues, tickets to the ballet, a rare and beautiful doll, or even a gift certificate to an exclusive shop known for "labels" and quality.

What about the guys, you say? Tell Libra to go fly a kite! This sign loves wind. How about a ride in a hot air balloon? This encompasses what Libra men tend to be attracted to and that is gorgeous scenery with a nagging element of danger. Casual shirts that are also colorful in terms of the sky—pale blue, indigo, aqua, ivory, and soft yellow go over well. A slim volume of poetry by Keats is certain to please this balanced sign. After all, Libra is a great lover of poetry and high-brow forms of literature. It is very important to the Libra individual to appear cultivated and refined. A silk shirt with a set of elegant cufflinks is ideal for the Libra man. Books about relationships (Libra's favorite subject), texts on the law, or books about famous court cases are the subjects Libra loves to devour. A compass and a set of scales are also great tools for Libra, the dual sign who is forever losing his way. Yet the greatest gift of all is helping Libra to come to a decision. Do this and it'll make Libra's day!

SCORPIO

Think *spooky*. Scorpios are scary. They are attracted to the extremes in life, preferring subjects that have some element of danger. Scorpio's danger is not overt. It can be very subtle, such as a fascination for the dark side of life. A good place to start would be to buy Scorpio a book of ghost stories or the latest novel by Anne Rice. Go to a shop and pick out something that spells out the word *gothic*—all in shades of crimson, pewter, and black. Speaking of gothic, books on the occult, ancient Egypt, magic spells, witchcraft, and unexplained mysteries all appeal to the imagination of a Scorpio. Scorpio also likes stories about famous murders and crimes and how they are eventually solved. Many Scorpios have a strong interest in the presidency, so biographies of U.S. presidents are sure to please your basic Scorpio—as long as he or she reads. If not, spend your bucks on a scary movie. All Scorpios love them.

The best birthday vacation for Scorpio is one where you both escape to New Orleans—and don't forget to buy Scorpio a voodoo doll! Speaking of voodoo dolls, Scorpio is forever interested in books and techniques on how to get revenge. No sign feels as slighted as a Scorpio. There are humorous books available on the subject of revenge so check them out. Another great choice for Scorpio would be a very old bottle of wine. The preferred taste is *red wine*, of course. Like Aries, Scorpio likes red—but not the burning red fires of passion that Aries prefers. Scorpio prefers *blood red*.

When you buy Scorpio an item of clothing, make sure the predominant color is black. Scorpio loves anything in crushable black velvet or black satin. Musk perfumes, aromatic oils, candles, copies of the *Kama Sutra*, sex manuals, and books on how to win and succeed are all excellent choices for a Scorpio. As far as jewel pieces are concerned, go for garnets, filigree, and smoky topaz. Gloves and boots are also romantic accessories for this charismatic sign. Scorpio prefers richness and mystery over items that are conventionally pretty.

The best thing you can give a Scorpio, however, is yourself clad in sexy new underwear. (Meeting Scorpio at the door nude isn't a bad idea, either.) Once again, black and red are the best colors. This brings up one of Scorpio's favorite games: chess. Like Aries, Scorpio aims to win but more in terms of mind control and strategy. Unlike Aries, Scorpio bides his time and waits for the perfect time to strike.

Other favorite games of Scorpio would be the game "Clue" and another game (which may not really be a game in any ordinary sense of the word) that would be the Ouija board. In this way, you and Scorpio can wile away the night talking with the spirits of the dead. Don't be afraid because you can be certain that Scorpio isn't!

SAGITTARIUS

This fiery Archer sign is not only a rebel, he is a clown. Sometimes Sagittarius is even a saint. So whenever you are buying for a

Sagittarius, you must always have these three identities in mind. Humorous cards and gag gifts are good choices early in the relationship, but cards with romantic themes or mushy sentiments make Sagittarius feel trapped, so avoid these in the beginning. (After you get to know Sagittarius more intimately, you may want to avoid the sentimental stuff entirely.) The saintly Sagittarius likes contemporary New Age books or videos that emphasize the spiritual in everyday life. It generally doesn't matter which religion the books cover. Sagittarius remains curious about them all.

Black leather pants, chaps, and jackets are favorites for Sagittarius. Denim clothing features in as a strong second choice. Sagittarians usually go for gifts that represent freedom on some level. Therefore, motorcycles, trampolines, bicycles, a carriage ride, or a day of horseback riding in the country are sure to please this mutable sign so fond of the great outdoors. Books on philosophy by contemporary authors such as Camille Paglia or Robert Bly are sure to please, as well as fiction by Kurt Vonnegut and Mark Twain. Books covering the lives of the saints will appeal to the zodiac's only horseman. Funny thing—horses appeal to him as well. Speaking of books, Sagittarius often has a hankering to become a published author himself, so a guidebook on how to write and sell your first book is an excellent choice for your Sagittarius.

A trip to the circus, the amusement park, or a party with a circus theme are certain to appeal to your average Sagittarius. When planning a party for Sagittarius, think of balloons, booze, confetti, and music by the Doors. Bring on the gourmet jelly beans, too, but forget the cake and ice cream: they don't go very well with beer. Also, invite every party animal that you know of, and as many as can fit in one room. Sagittarius thrives on fun. You might also consider one of those new beer-brewing kits. The kid's game "Twister" is another hands-down winner.

Amethyst is the select gem of most Sagittarians and so are the colors purple and reddish brown. A deck of Tarot cards or books about religion, most especially early Christianity or Buddhism, will appeal to the curious but structured imagination of Sagittarius. This sign loves to rebel against the status quo but within certain constraints. Early in life, Sagittarius lives an existence that is like a page torn out of a biography of Jim Morrison. Later in life, it is not unusual for Sagittarius to become conventionally religious. It's important to appeal to these various sides when choosing gifts—the rebel, the clown, and the saint—for this free-wheeling, unusual Fire sign.

CAPRICORN

Admittedly, it's difficult to buy a gift for a person who has so much in common with Ebenezer Scrooge. Just make certain that whatever you buy Capricorn is somewhat usable and practical. Avoid the bows and frills—go for quality. Capricorns are forever striving and working. They seldom want to ease back and have some fun. After all, they don't want to lose the power and ground they feel they've gained. Capricorns tend to get drunk on power; this is what drives them. Capricorn is a sign that works and manipulates to build his own kingdom on earth. He is afraid that if he takes his eye off the ball, he will lose it all.

Capricorns tend to be attracted to things that relate to the time of year around their birthdays. Therefore, interesting gift choices might be a snow globe, a pair of ice skates, snow tires, or a set of tiny lights to string in the bare trees. Like Cancer, Capricorn is tied to the past and thus appreciates antiques or something that is just old with an interesting history—this typically means American history. Books about royalty or medieval times, as well as guides to financial success, always attracts the sign that is eager to rub shoulders with either the important or the rich. Like Leos, Capricorns find it in their destinies to *impress*.

Money clips, an expensive leather bag, a gold pocket watch, or a paperweight engraved with Capricorn's name are sure to flatter this sign of the Wintry Goat. A special message or card received from someone rich or powerful is bound to delight even the most dour Capricorn. So think of someone famous you know! Imported cigars, a piggy bank, gloves lined with fur, and books with tips about the stock market or tips on gardening make excellent gifts for this fussy Earth sign.

Clocks are also items of curiosity for the average Capricorn. Buy your Capricorn a timepiece in either an antique shop or a very fine store with imported clocks. The more the clock ticks and tocks, the more Capricorn loves it! Other ideal gifts would be the collected works of Edgar Allan Poe; clothing in charcoal gray, navy, or brown; or a picture book of old historical cemeteries. Capricorn is the sign of measure and time. So make time for your Capricorn!

AQUARIUS

First of all, be certain that your present for Aquarius is *very* unusual. Go out and look for the strangest, rarest gift you can find. Telescopes are a good beginning. So are the latest computer technology and software. Videos and books with science-fiction themes always go over well. Strange literary works, such as books by William S. Burroughs, Harlan Ellison, or bestsellers about weird kinky cults generally appeal to your well-read Aquarian. Numerous places would be perfect getaway vacations for Aquarius. The two that spring to mind are Roswell, New Mexico, and Disney World.

Let's just say that Aquarians are attracted to things that are on the fringe of polite society. In other words, ordinary life bores them. This makes your Aquarius both easy and hard to buy for. The easy part is, go for the strangest thing you can spot in the store. The hard part is, you'll have to hunt for a store that has borderline bizarre and quirky gift items. Bookstores are the best place to start. Comic books with fantasy or science-fiction themes appeal to Aquarius. Serious books on odd sexual practices also appeal to Aquarians, such as stories about the lives of transsexuals and biographies of people who have lived their lives to the extreme, such as the Marquis de Sade or Catherine the Great.

Those born under the sign of Aquarius wish to be taken to other worlds—either in a rocket ship or just in their imaginations. They prefer movies with the most elaborate visual effects and the most technological appeal. Aquarian women are attracted to clothing that looks more like "costuming." They go for gypsy scarves, velvet gloves, vests, textured stockings, and either long or very short skirts. For Aquarian guys, buy a black shirt with interesting buttons, or black suede boots with high heels. Aquarian guys prefer to dress like matadors, Men-in-Black, or David Duchovny. Lava lamps, movies or posters with high-tech monsters, neon-glow stars and planets that you stick to the ceiling, music by Jon Anderson, or merely the latest craze or gadget are likely to please Aquarius and keep him occupied.

The latest New Age wisdom book or new divination games are other easy favorites for those born under the Water-Bearer sign.

Probably one of the best gifts is to have your Aquarian's horo-scope cast. He'll claim he doesn't believe in astrology, yet this will fascinate him. In a pinch, look for a gift that fits Aquarius best—*something odd and truly rare.*

PISCES

Think *moods*. You can be certain Pisces has plenty of them. Buy Pisces a journal to write down his thoughts. Also, look for books on art and poetry, books on how to make masks and costumes, books about angels or Edgar Cayce, books on how to read auras, or the journals of diarist Anaïs Nin. Get Pisces a flowing cape or a cloak lined in dark blue satin. Buy a tie that includes rainbows or the colors of the ocean. Floating candles in shades of lilac and indigo, good luck charms, jewelry with religious symbols, oils, and aromatherapy are sure to please your Fish in the sea. Purple is usually the Pisces' favorite color so keep your eye tuned in when browsing and trying to find the most purplish present that you can!

On that special day, treat your Pisces to some wine and caviar or a seafood dinner. Light plenty of candles to set a certain mood. Get comfortable and give your Pisces an impromptu psychic read-ing. Stay positive. Pisceans can be very impressionable. Take Pisces to a palm-reader or a reflexologist. They love that sort of thing. After all, Pisces is the sign of the feet and there is nothing more delightful than getting a foot massage or a new pair of shoes. Pisceans are attracted to very unusual shoes, like those clear plexiglass shoes that resemble Cinderella slippers. Pisceans are also attracted to footware that looks like ballet slippers in cushy velvet. Costuming is as important to Pisces as it is to Aquarius, but Pisces has more of a sense of romanticism and the past, whereas Aquarius is a bit wild and nervy.

A string of pearls, a neckpiece made of crystals, or mood rings are ideal gifts for Pisces. Books on fairies and angels, spirituality best-sellers, clothing with rainbows or sequins, music that is softly evocative, seashells, Dove chocolates, and Victorian gazing balls all appeal to this receptive water sign. The best gifts you can give Pisces, though, are a full body massage and lots of emotional support. All in all, Pisces people prefer things that remind them of the spiritual in every-day life. Pisces understands the power of the human soul as a part of a greater source. The perfect gift for those born under the sign of the Mermaids is one that reminds them of our connection to something greater than ourselves—to Pisces, that is the most welcome gift of all.

In relationships of every kind, the gifts we give to show our love are essential and significant. Picking the right kind of gift is important, not because our loved ones expect gifts but because we show through our gifts how much we understand our lovers and respect their interests—interests that may be quite different from our own. Giving the perfect gift to your perfect love becomes easy once you understand the fundamental natures of the twelve astro-logical signs. Then, gift giving is a pleasure—and a breeze!

FIVE

THE STORY OF THE "O"

Orgasm happens in the mind; at least, this is what sex researchers have told us for the past thirty-five years or so. Astrologers know better. Sex happens throughout the body, as well as in the mind, the soul, and the spirit of the individual. All the senses are included, even those we may not know about yet. The outer framework of the body corresponds to the twelve signs of the zodiac. Whatever astrological sign you are born under determines the area of your body that needs the most stimulation during sex. Then, of course, your mind, your reactions, your soul, and the connection you feel with your lover all factor into the equation.

We are a goal-oriented society. This may be why people go nuts over sexual satisfaction and orgasm in our culture. Humans revolve around the God of Sex like planets revolve around the sun. Naturally, reaching orgasm is essential to having a fully satisfying relationship. If one person enjoys orgasm while the other does not, the relationship may not be as balanced as we would like. Work needs to be done.

Typically, in lovemaking we believe that our partners like what we do sexually; and it's true that if we enjoy sex, our partners will as well. At the same time, the zodiac signs are quite different from each other. Some like fast, whistle-stop sex, reaching orgasm quickly, while other signs take it slow and allow plenty of time to see what "comes." If people with these two different energies are married or entwined in a serious relationship, one person will invariably end up resentful.

Of course, once you understand astrology, this incompatibility can be avoided because you already know what your lover wants. You know that Aries prefers sex to be fast and rough, and Taurus likes it slow. You realize that Leo must feel adored in order to get off, while Virgo needs to believe that both of you are being just a little bit naughty before he can keep his Virgo rising. Human beings are very complicated, and not one is the same as another. There are variations of truth even within the ancient framework of astrology.

As far as sexual gratification goes, however, understanding the signs can certainly point you in the right direction. It is a rare person, indeed, who claims to have nothing in common with the personality traits of his birth sign. Yet astrology goes well beyond the personality. The influence of the stars is just as strong in governing not only the physical appearance but also the responses of the body. Each zodiac sign rules parts of the body that in turn create a galaxy of sexual sensations, physical traits, and functions.

Do you have an inkling of what the most sensitive and responsive parts of your lover's body might be? Here is a brief summary of the zodiac signs and the parts of the human body they rule. Touch your lover there and see what develops.

- ARIES: This Fire sign rules the head, ears, and parts of the neck. Aries likes having his scalp manipulated, his hair pulled, and his ears nibbled during sex.

- TAURUS: This Earth sign rules the neck and pectorals. Lick Taurus in both areas. Bite at him a little. Moan softly against his throat, growl, and hum a sexy tune.

- GEMINI: This Air sign rules the hands, the forearms, the mouth, and the eyes. That gives you a lot of territory to cover. Use your tongue proficiently. Oral sex or hand jobs are deeply appreciated. Gemini usually comes pretty quickly.

- CANCER: This Water sign rules the breasts and she has the mammaries to prove it. Cancer women can be brought to orgasm just by manipulating their breasts. Men like this almost as well, so lick and kiss their nipples during the peak moments of sex.

- LEO: This Fire sign rules the heart and the chest as well, which means Leo likes sex with great gusto and energy. Wrestle, struggle, or have a lot of foreplay before sex to get Leo's heart up to speed. His orgasm will be incredible.

- VIRGO: This Earth sign rules the lower abdomen and inner thighs. Part the legs of Virgo firmly and fall between them. Swiftly kiss the stomach and inner thighs. Give Virgo time to catch his or her breath and then penetrate deeply. It'll drive Virgo mad!

- LIBRA: This Air sign rules the pubic bone. Pay as much attention to that area as you can, while whispering sweet nothings in the cracks. Pull at the buttocks before you push.

- SCORPIO: This Water sign rules the genitals and anus. Wait! It's not as bad as it sounds! Just pay as much attention to the underside of Scorpio's genitals as to the upper side. (Also, some Scorpios really do like anal sex.)

- SAGITTARIUS: This Fire sign rules the buttocks and the thighs, as well as the pelvis. Hold onto that butt for dear life, then move in a grinding, circular motion. Use the same movements as the most masterful belly dancer does. Sagittarius will love it!

- CAPRICORN: This Earth sign rules the spine, knees, and skin. Capricorn likes the feeling of being completely enclosed and held during sex. Soothing massage concentrating on the backs of the calves, the upper back, and then the stomach and breasts usually arouses this staid sign to the point of no return.

- AQUARIUS: This Air sign traditionally rules the shins; however, Aquarius actually governs the central nervous system, so this means the most erogenous zones for Aquarians are the brain and all over the entire body! Keep this sign visually stimulated during sex. Also, play music or make love by the light of a big TV screen. You get the picture.

- PISCES: This Water sign rules the feet and the auric field. (What else?) Pisces governs what can't be seen through ordinary vision. People born under this sign do love having their feet manipulated, though. They also love being kissed around the nose and eyes. Blending pure, spiritual essences during intimate acts makes sex with Pisces a mind-blowing experience.

Now that you know which body parts to pay attention to when making love with your partner, read the following descriptions to get the entire picture of what sex with your lover might be like. Here are a few sign traits and suggestions.

ARIES

Lovemaking should be vigorous, fast, and rough. Aries doesn't mind a bit of wailing and back scratching; in fact, he actually prefers it. Squirming, struggling to get away, and strong rocking motions turn this guy on like nothing else. Aries women want sex to be like an invigorating game of tennis, with sweat, cursing, and blood and guts. Sexual positions should resemble the positions in touch football. Expect few tender moments—everything is a face-off and a fight to the finish with all of the jeers and cheers! In moments of passion, pull on Aries' hair *really hard*! Sober him up by hitting his head into headboard of the bed and then slap him hard on the ass. Start to push Aries away roughly, then turn around and pull him inside you just as aggressively. This will catch Aries off-guard. He loves that! Wrestle the Aries woman on top of you lickety-split, grab some hair on top of her head, and penetrate her deeply. As she yowls and begs for more, don't stop pumping until she collapses into orgasms and melts over you like a fine, panting mist.

At times, Aries will come *too quickly* so it's important not to strongly stimulate Aries too early in the lovemaking sessions. Some Aries women come as quickly as the men do. Aries finds sex highly exhilarating as exercise. They love it and need it frequently and will grow resentful if deprived or turned down too often.

TAURUS

Don't nod off under this one. Taurus takes a long time, but stay with him and you will enjoy the entire experience. Sex with the Bull is often warm and soothing. Taurus needs lots of foreplay but with relaxed, delectable moves. Go slow and easy at first, then get gradually rougher. Make sure to nuzzle and bite at the neck and ears. Pretend to be Count Dracula for a few minutes. This will give

Taurus a huge thrill. The neck and pectoral muscles are highly erogenous zones for Taureans of both sexes. Tongue and suck the Adam's Apple quite gently. Kiss his eyes and chin.

Many Taureans prefer the behind position, and the majority love big rear ends, so keep your buttocks in the air or at least in view. Don't be bashful. Show him what you have. Give orders and say what you need. Be explicit. Taurus will be pleased if you tell him exactly what to do. Taking orders turns him on.

Taurus expects steady, reliable sex. The Bull usually goes for straight sex but is open to suggestions. He prefers his lovers to be grounded but to also have an imagination. Taurus men are famous for being quite well endowed, and both sexes like body parts to be large. Taurus men go for meaty women, and Taurus women go for the same. The Taurus woman, however, looks for a man with a penis the size of a bull's. One plus is the fact that you needn't be ashamed of your body around a Taurus. They easily forgive flaws, and when it comes to sex, they aren't too particular.

Taurus is the sign of the appetite so Taurus needs a great deal of sexual gratification. Without it, he becomes grouchy. Taurus is an excellent lover as long as you don't rush things. Lovemaking with a Taurus can go on for an entire lazy afternoon.

Gemini

As the sign of versatility and quicksilver, Gemini has an added bonus when it comes to love and sex. Gemini rules the hands, the mouth, and the tongue. Think *oral*, if you're wondering how to delight Gemini in the bedroom. Gemini's tongue is the most deft and sensitive part of his body, even more dexterous than his amazing fingers.

Deep kissing and oral sex provide some of the greatest pleasures with your Gemini lover. Kissing a Gemini is incredible. He has the fastest, most talented lips around. Hand jobs through the clothing are immensely exciting, too, so you can take your pleasure as lovers even when riding in the back of a taxicab or stealing behind staircases and doorways.

Thrill your Gemini lover by calling a friend while you're having sex—but don't dare mention this to the friend, or it will break the spell. Gemini loves to take dares and risks. When you're away from each other, don't be afraid to indulge in phone sex. The practice of phone sex is a Gemini thing. In fact, a Gemini probably invented phone sex since Gemini is the sign most affected by the voice.

Kissing is even more of a turn-on for Gemini than for other signs so plan to kiss and tongue for while before going a bit farther. In fact, the kisses and caresses of a Gemini can bring on an orgasm, but don't waste it. Put your tongue in Gemini's ears while you caress the groin area. Talk somewhat raunchy to Gemini during the sex act. Moan and scream a little more than is usual for you. The most erogenous zone for Gemini is a sharp and well-honed mind. Without a mind connection, the sex will be less incredible. At the same time, be open to experimentation and to bringing in another person. After all, Gemini shares everything—including *his sex*!

CANCER

The sign of the Crab has the greatest set of mammaries on the planet. Remember actress Jayne Mansfield, the brown-eyed Marilyn

Monroe? Her breasts spilled out of her dress at a fancy awards dinner in Hollywood in the early 1960s. TV stations had to put a
black bar across her chest, but gorgeous Jayne just kept on jig-
gling. Mansfield had Cancer Rising in her chart. If Cancer isn't
born with a great set, she'll pay big money for them—hence,
Cancer native Pamela Anderson.

The point is that the breasts are the most highly erogenous
zone for Cancer natives—this includes both men and women born
under the sign.

Treat Cancer's breasts like succulent fruit. Nibble a while, but
every so gently as Cancer is ultra-sensitive in the chest region! As
you suck and fondle the breasts, massage the pubic area more stri-
dently. Hold Cancerians firmly because they like the feeling of
being overcome. This will probably bring Cancer to orgasm right
then and there.

Cancer men are also sensitive in the breast area. They lift a lot
of weights to build up their chests. Play into this erogenous zone
by straddling the Cancer man, kissing and sucking his nipples while
having intercourse. Pump rhythmically with your pelvis while blow-
ing against his face and neck. Cancer loves the idea of you doing
all the work. Move into other areas as well, the throat, the ribcage,
and the stomach, another sexually excitable region for Cancer!

Make Cancer feel desirable by being the one most interested
in taking charge.

LEO

Leo is a sign that desires and expects adulation in all areas of
romance, but most especially sex. Therefore, when making love to

Leo, act as if you are only there for his or her pleasure. Use your body in worshipful motions as if praying while kissing Leo's groin area. Make lots of noise with Leo and whip yourself around. Cat sounds are best. Make sure you squirm, moan, and tell Leo how great he is. (Use restraint while doing this; in other words, don't flatter him to the point that Leo thinks he's too good for you.)

Use as many mirrors as you can find around your lovemaking area, including lots of candles to cast a warm light—just enough to create a special glow on your writhing bodies. Make sure you're in pretty good shape, too. If not, wear suggestive attire: clouds of veils, underwear without a crotch, or a sexy girdle that leaves the genitals exposed.

With Leo, sex is a dance, a game of give and take. Growl and purr against Leo's heart area, as this is where his sexual power is. Make certain your lovemaking is a little vigorous, enough to keep the blood rushing. Show Leo you have animal strength as a lover. Act as if you are a fountain of sexual power. Hold your own against Leo.

The more Leo believes you are impressed with his lovemaking, the more he will stay inspired and the better lover he will become. Leo's problem is his vanity. He tends to collect beautiful and vapid lovers with a lot of space between their ears. Demonstrate to Leo that lovers who are his equal make the best lovers of all. Let Leo know that you have a lot of sexual fortitude, as well as a lot of *heart*.

VIRGO

Secretly, Virgo is a very horny sign. He thinks about sex all of the time but feels guilty over his compulsion. This is why you find lots of Virgo in the natal charts of individuals who have a sexual addiction. As a child, Virgo was made to feel that nice people don't have sex, or at least, the nice people Virgo knows don't have sex, such as his parents, teachers, and Bible preachers.

Such repressive ideas bring out a kind of sexual hedonism once Virgo leaves home. Since sex is taboo, Virgo can't get enough of it. Sex is always in the back of the mind of even the most inhibited Virgo. It's sort of like the old phrase, "I forbid you to think about pink elephants!" So what does Virgo think about? Pink elephants, of course.

To keep Virgo excited, you must cautiously play into his naughty fantasies, which are really rather tame. Don't tell Virgo that his fantasies are tame, though; he will lose his sexual excitement. Parade around Virgo in explicit clothes, rub his crotch, then pose in somewhat vulgar ways. Usually, this isn't much more than doing the tango in black underwear while clamping a rose between your teeth. Just remember: *Bad! You two are being very bad!*

Virgo should be seduced gradually, so don't make any quick or unexpected moves. In the midst of "partaking of the forbidden fruit" with your particular Virgo, make sure you concentrate on the stomach and groin area. Parting the legs and licking the inner thighs of Virgo works like a charm. Then make snarling sounds as if you are going to eat up his genitals. Blow raspberries on his stomach. Just act dominant and in control.

Later, a relaxing massage works to calm Virgo, who is usually rather tense. Words of encouragement mixed in with a few lewd sexual commands will keep your Virgo rising.

LIBRA

Avoid any vulgarity right off the bat. There is nothing that turns a Libran off as much as a dirty mouth. Don't get me wrong, Libra likes a bit of erotic talk as long as it is tasteful. After all, Libra is governed by Venus, planet of lovers. Venus is also the ruler of artful porn. Vampire author Anne Rice is a Libra, which is surprising if you haven't read her erotica books. They're not in bad taste, but there are still plenty of parts to turn you on. Libra loves sex as much as anyone; Libra just wants it to be pretty, if not a bit decadent.

What excites Libra? Making love on satin sheets with ripples of classical music in the background. Music with harps and violins is *perfect*! So is endearing talk and sweet smelling oils with lots and lots of candles in the room. When you think of Libra, just think of ambience. Why not drape veils around your bed to make a beautiful enclosure? Use mountains and mountains of pillows when you're having sex.

The funny thing is, Librans seem to enjoy sex in close proximity to crowds. Go outside naked except for your coat. Making love in a closet outside a room filled with people is certain to add that element of danger Libra delights in. Having sex in the bathroom at a party is also thrilling for this usually tame sign.

When you're alone, treat Libra with an impromptu striptease or suggest that Libra strip. Slip a twenty inside Libra's underwear and then tell him to earn it. Kiss Libra around his butt crack and nibble at those darling dimples above each cheek. Go for Libra's pubic area, kiss and lick, do a little oral work, and then stop abruptly. When Libra wants more, straddle him, and order your Libra to finish the work you started. Make sure you smell like a passionfruit, a flower, or a French whore. Libra has fantasies of domination, with whips and chains, so play into this. Buy a few sex toys and present them to Libra. Ask Libra how to use them and he'll show you. *Oooooh, will he ever!*

SCORPIO

How to arouse a Scorpio? Just part your legs a little and give Scorpio a long, burning stare. This sign is into intensity and what sexual intensity can bring, including hours and hours of incredible sex. Despite what the dime-store astrology books say about Scorpio, don't expect your Scorpio to be sex-obsessed. After all, Scorpio is the master of control, and sex is just one of the many things Scorpio easily masters.

What does he do with all of this bottled-up sexual energy? He saves it for the next lover, and then the next. Scorpios aren't into "quickies" or one-night stands. They want every sexual experience to be fully gratifying—passionate evenings filled with kissing and grinding. Sex is like wrestling to Scorpio. Basically, he'll wear you out and only then give you a gift of precious orgasm. Scorpio wants to make sure you remember him!

Scorpio is the sign that rules the genitals, so expect no problems there. Scorpios come as quickly or as slowly as they choose. The unusual thing about Scorpio women is that some ejaculate just like men. Incredibly, they spurt during orgasm! It can be a bit unnerving to men who aren't aware of this. So after a petting session with Scorpio, don't be surprised if you have to change your clothes. Scorpios are pretty high on sexual fluids. This may sound made-up, but it isn't. It's just one of the many curiosities about the sign.

Scorpio revels in mystery, taboo, and intrigue. Scorpios prefer elements of danger in their sexual exploits—not in Libra's make-believe fashion, but by actually doing scary, daring things. If you don't like that, however, Scorpio won't make you participate. Scorpio prefers his sexual sessions to be long and fabulous. Keep in mind that when bedding a Scorpio, you're having sex with the best stinger around.

SAGITTARIUS

This is one rowdy lover, with the greatest looking ass you can imagine. For those who thrive on thrills (the kind of cheap, screaming thrills you get on a roller-coaster ride to hell and back), Sagittarius is the one to wrap your legs around and strap yourself onto. With a Sagittarius, you can have fun sex with no strings attached.

Sex is a good workout with Sagittarius, so consider starting out by wrestling naked. The more you roll around and end up outside in the yard or humping on the kitchen table, the better it is. Come to think of it, Sagittarius loves stealing a bit of afternoon delight in the great outdoors. So the best thing to do is to drive up into the mountains one day to mount your summits of sexual pleasure. (The City Park will only attract crowds of the curious.) Skinny-dipping is a great sexual stimulator for Sagittarians. (They probably invented it.)

Sagittarius rules the buttocks and thighs. (The sign of the Archer goes for big butts, so that's a plus for many of us.) It goes without saying that the powerful legs and butt of this nature girl or boy will help you reach your peak experience.

Sexually, Sagittarius prefers lovers who are strong and physically fit, but this doesn't mean skinny. Sagittarius prefers lovers with bodies that are meaty but compact, and those who treat sex like an invigorating hike in the woods.

What Sagittarius dislikes are passive lovers, those who stay in one spot, waiting to be pampered and pleasured. Are you into sexual adventure? Prepare to go on a marathon romp with your Sagittarian love and scale the summits of erotic bliss.

CAPRICORN

Capricorns were born in the wrong century. They tend to have old-fashioned sexual values. They prefer having sex with the lights out and probably through their nightgowns. If you can get them over their insecurities and self-repression, Capricorns make lovers with great imagination and endurance.

Like Virgo, Capricorn strains under the burden of his sexuality, but when he cuts loose he goes for it all. What starts out as great inhibition can end up as total hedonism, as radio shock jock Howard Stern (who, not surprisingly, is a Capricorn) represents. No other sign can be as gluttonous about sexual matters as a Capricorn. No other sign can be as preoccupied or base about sensual matters. This is just Capricorn attempting to escape the Inquisition of his childhood. Someone far back in Capricorn's past told him that sex was wrong. Therefore, sex is now as much of a thrill as stealing.

The real truth is that Capricorn has problems with intimacy, so naturally the most intimate act of all will suffer. Typically, Capricorn prefers plain, straight-on sex unless taught otherwise. So it's important to discuss and make plans for sex

with your Capricorn love by making suggestions about what you
need and like.

Capricorn is turned on by what is denied, so he has lavish fantasies of illicit affairs. It's important to play into these fantasies by
sneaking a bit of sexual action here and there. Buy erotic books and
tapes, then enjoy them together. Initiate sex with Capricorn. He'll be
very grateful if you do. Sexuality must evolve, however, rather than
the two of you indulging in any monkey business on your first date.

Breaking out of a routine works best for Capricorn sexually.
Having sex in a different place each time will do much to spice
up your love life. Capricorn is a "leg man." He adores great legs
and short skirts. Keep this in mind. Capricorn women prefer men
with *enormous* . . . wallets of course! Give Capricorn plenty of
good loving, for he has mountains to climb. Together, the world
and every imaginable pleasure will be yours!

AQUARIUS

They were the first ones to get their tongues and belly buttons
pierced. Does this tell you anything? Aquarians simply like oddness, and, of course, this carries over into their sexual preferences.
Aquarians want to do something *different* from everyone else; thus,
their sexual affairs will be quite unorthodox. Bisexuality, as well as
S & M, may figure in, but not always.

So to sexually excite and fulfill your Aquarius love, the greatest tool you can use is your imagination. This may mean going a
little *bizarro* on your Aquarius—like showing up for your date
with a suitcase full of sex toys and wearing a wig of grassy green
hair. Keep in mind that Aquarius loves gadgets, contraptions, and

anything new (especially if it's off-limits), so toys will be met with great eagerness. He also likes things that promise taboo sexual experiences, so keep your bullwhip handy.

In many ways the psychedelic era was tailor-made for Aquarians. For this reason, anything evoking that "live and let live" period such as lava lamps, videos with surging patterns and lights, and even disco balls, are wonderful to make love by. Another excellent way of arousing Aquarius is to suggest that you dress in each other's clothes and "make out" while slowly undressing each other. Gender-bending is a great turn-on for the Water-Bearer sign. He'll never admit to it, of course so make it a game and just don't call it that.

Aquarius likes sex to be a bit faster than the rest of the signs. If you spend a great deal of time talking, then making love, then talking again, it will bring on the closeness that Aquarius needs in a love or sex mate.

Keep in mind that Aquarius is in love with the strange. So if Aquarius says he's after something strange, just tell him that *you* *are*. Look forward to what develops as a result.

PISCES

Illusions and psychological traps turn on sexually complex Pisces. Pisces can be a seductive sign but is also easily seduced—perhaps being "sucked in" is a more accurate expression. Pisces is highly impressionable and tends to go along with just about anything as long as others are "doing it." Pisces is the sign of the martyr and the saint, and is considered to be a rather "easy lay."

Within reason, Pisces will follow just about anything you suggest, but if you want sex and are too shy to ask, Pisces will intuit your intent and probably do the seducing first. Pisces loves "atmosphere," so candles, aromatherapy, and scented oils should figure into your lovemaking. Pisces also rules the feet. Both male and female Pisces adore shoes and feet, and you will find that many Pisceans develop foot fetishes. So when you are involved in seducing or being seduced, make certain you bring sexy shoes, garter belts, and suggestive hosiery as a part of your lovemaking routine.

Although Pisces has a strong tendency toward being spiritual, Pisces also loves sex—but to a Pisces, sex is like a dream that floats in and out of consciousness. Yet it is a dream that Pisces is not particularly attached to. Therefore, you will have to lead Pisces by the outer limits of your sexual imagination.

If Pisces is still inhibited, consider getting both of you a bit tipsy, but avoid hard alcohol. Pisces is an inordinately sensitive sign. Pisceans' most erogenous zone is their skin, but they have no special spot for you to concentrate on—just make love longingly and deliciously. Pisces is a fast learner when it comes to sex, and keep in mind that the sign of Mermaids and martyrs makes the most sensual lovers of all.

Reaching orgasm only takes imagination and knowledge of the twelve astrological signs. While some signs are easily aroused, others require a little more patience and work. Our sexuality is mapped out in our horoscopes from birth and thus is easily read by expert astrologers. If you want more detailed information about your sexuality and your lover's, or if you have problems, consider having your natal horoscopes cast and interpreted by a master astrologer.

Whether we are a prince, movie star, or pauper, what we like in the bedroom can be interpreted by the most cursory glance at the natal horoscope. Learn the knowledge of the stars. Open your world to incredible sex and learn to make love yours!

SIX

THE RISING SIGN AND ROMANCE: WAYS TO BED, WED, AND KEEP THE EGO FED

The Rising sign has to do with the time of day you were born. It takes the Sun twenty-four hours to glide across the twelve astrological signs, which are clustered stars or constellations. We know that the Sun comes up over the eastern horizon each morning. Although we cannot see them, the constellations, along with their houses and astrological signs, continue to rise (or, at least, from earth they appear to) just like the wheels on a mechanical timepiece. Thus, whatever House or constellation was rising at the time you were born constitutes your Rising sign.

For instance, if you were born under the sign of Taurus, at exactly daybreak the constellation Taurus will be rising. Two hours later, the Gemini constellation will be rising. If you were born with a Scorpio birthday, though, the time of year would be different. So naturally, at daybreak, your Rising sign would be Scorpio. With the seasons, it gradually changes from month to month. Still confused? Included is a table to help you find your Rising signs and your lover's.

So, what is the Rising sign and how important is it to romance? The Rising sign is the Mask of Self that the world sees. Often, the first impression we give others is that of our Rising sign. In astrology, the Rising sign is also the First House, also known as the House of Self. It is our outer projection of self. Directly opposite the First House, or Rising sign, is the Seventh House of Partners and Marriage. You can consider these houses two sides of the same mirror, only colored somewhat differently; however, the First House is "you" while the Seventh House is "everyone else," but most specifically life partners and the people we are most compatible with. This is why the Seventh House has been traditionally called the House of Marriage.

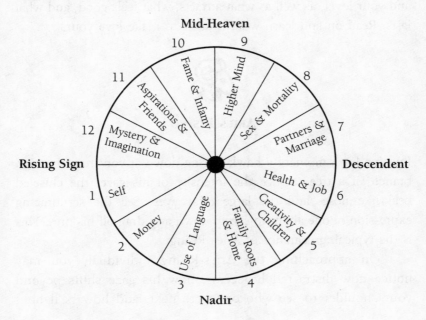

In looking at the horoscopes of individuals, ancient stargazers noticed that opposite signs attract. Yet even more than an individual's Sun sign, their Rising sign seemed most important in determining what makes a relationship work. Therefore, when we look at the Rising sign as a clue to compatibility, its opposite sign, known as the descendant or Seventh House, is the one that appears to govern how long a relationship will last or whether it is meant to last at all.

Other factors figure in, such as Moon signs, Venus signs, and Mars signs. One simple way of determining compatibility in a romantic relationship is to go beyond your Sun sign and your lover's and learn about the harmonics found between Sun signs, Moon signs, and Rising signs. Put them all together and see how they match up with your own. After all, the Rising sign and the Seventh House influence the level of compatibility between you and your lover, as well as what attracts, what feels good, and what lasts. Read on and learn what it takes to make love yours.

ARIES RISING

Imagine for a moment a hawk staring down at you from the high branch of a tree. Notice the intensity of his gaze, the chiseled beak-like nose, and the large clear eyes. See the scrutinizing expression of one about to sweep down and drag off his prey. This is the typical appearance of Aries Rising.

On approaching the Aries-Rising individual, you may notice how distracted he seems, how his gaze shifts beyond your shoulder to see who or what's next, and how he'll hold his ground. Aries is forever poised for his next challenge, always chomping at the bit. Perhaps you'll notice the large, proud head or a strangely shaped skull with bumps on the forehead like devil's horns. There may be a tendency toward scarring on the skin, or wrinkles that have formed from wearing a worried expression.

Aries Rising is not a romantic sign and is certainly not chivalrous. Thus, any relationship you might have with this Rising sign will have passion but with mostly unromantic elements. Aries is the sign of the foe and the opposition; therefore, all of his relationships are colored by this attitude. Aries is first and foremost a competitor and has difficulty understanding people who do not have the same attitude. Aries is greatly puzzled by people who allow him to walk all over them! Never allow this. If you do, he will leave you.

Even in the face of civility, Aries is aggressive and ready to meet the challenge. He makes a burning and intense lover, all the while not going in for sentimentality. This can be a crushing blow to those who expect poetry and romance. Oh, Aries Rising will do what he supposes he ought to, but the mushy aspects of romance are for the other birds, not him.

Aries-Rising women are slightly more romantic, because of cultural conditioning, and they love sex. Even Aries Amazons, however, are no-nonsense types, not into playing games in which you must prove how in love you both are. Either sex would rather be outside in nature, taking a hike, going for a run, or hitting a ball. If you want true action with an Aries, it must be out on a playing field. Aries people often love sports more than they do sex. Sports is a straight-on concept that this Aries understands. One wins and one loses. What could be simpler? The complications of romance and sex are what keep poor Aries befuddled.

When you are romantically involved with Aries Rising, never become intimidated. This will inspire him or her to be cruel or belittling. Act confident of your own abilities. Only when you face a lover with Aries Rising head-on will you earn his respect. Get used to his tendency toward brashness or loudness. Talk with him about his favorite subjects: himself and his current projects. Show him your strength, either in body or in mind. Better yet, show him that you are strong in both.

To Bed: To keep Aries crazy in love, attracted, and coming back for more, start off with some game or competition in which you oppose each other one-on-one, such as tennis, chess, or arm wrestling. Let this feeling of competition spill over into intimate small talk as if you are war buddies after winning your battle. Draw close, put your heads together, and laugh. Rub his ears and pull at his hair. Stare him dead straight in the eye, but don't get too mushy. This is one of the few things that scares the hell out of an Aries—the feeling of being head-over-heels in love.

To Wed: Not an easy feat! As the relationship progresses, allow Aries Rising see that you are great at making decisions. Although Aries looks at the big picture, he is not always great at coming to a decision. Be decisive and a leader to Aries. Stick fast to your decisions as long as they are sound and not too kooky. Show Aries that you are even more of an achiever than he is. Cultivate your powers of domination. Of course, all of this applies to women with Aries Rising as well.

To Keep the Ego Fed: Remind Aries Rising of all his or her wonderful wins and victories; however, never bring up the losses.

What Aries Rising Needs and Looks for in a Partner: What Aries looks for in a partner is culture and refinement. Aries is a visceral sign and often has very primitive drives and responses. Aries feels little shame over his aggressions. He thinks everyone has them to the same degree. In this way, Aries needs to be civilized, needs to learn how to keep his aggression in check. So, when looking at the polarity of Aries Rising, we find the sign Libra in his Seventh House of Marriage and Partners. Libra is the sign of the artist, the civilized, cultured human being. Libra, like Aries, is a driven sign but makes fewer enemies along the way. This is because Libra, unlike Aries, is tactful. Therefore, the best partner for Aries Rising would be a person with his or her Sun, and other planets, in the genteel and highly sophisticated sign of Libra.

Taurus Rising

This Rising sign is an artist and a wonderful sensualist. Look for a long swan-like neck or a thick Bull's torso. The voice is always "interesting." Either it grates or is as clear as bells. Taurus Rising is often is the sign of the singer. Think of Barbra Streisand. She sings with a crystal-clear voice. Think of Cher. She sings. That doesn't mean she has to carry a tune.

Though Taurus is often thought to be a proponent of traditional values and conservative opinions, the basic truth is that Taurus resists change. He has trouble with the new and different, but this doesn't mean he won't eventually accept it. It's just that he is stubborn and does not act quickly, especially when the changes are unexpected. Many times, things must be "perfect" before they can be acted upon, so everything seems very long and drawn out. This is because Taurus-Rising people are deliberate in action and thought, which means they tend to be purposely slow. The more you try to rush someone with Taurus Rising, the slower they become. Hasten a Taurus, and he or she will resist you. This is meant to get your goat so that you won't rush your Taurus anymore. Do not hurry this sign because he or she will only grow to resent you.

What Taurus Rising is looking for in a mate is someone physically attractive but also sexual and highly stimulating. After all, Taurus is ruled by Venus, planet of beauty and vanity, and thus is sensitive to the way things look. Taurus Rising doesn't mind taking a back seat so his lover can shine, but he wants to know that you appreciate all that he does for you. Also, get used to this sign demanding to be pampered every now and then. Taurus Rising fluctuates between wanting to be the parent and wanting to be the child. They don't mind that their lovers are getting all of the attention; they just want people to know that *they* are the driving force behind their lovers' successes.

In general, money means a lot to people born with Taurus Rising. They like to have plenty of money, and they like to spend it, too. Overspending is a great vice of Taurus Rising. Many end up in bankruptcy court. In keeping with this love of money and things, they like to be around others who are rich or privileged, perhaps in the hopes that some of the wealth will rub off on them. Nevertheless, Taurus Rising doesn't love money as much as he loves the sexual chase.

Taurus is a highly sexual sign, and this Rising sign typically exudes a great deal of sexual charisma to the opposite sex. Usually you can tell Taurus Rising from her classic dress with a plunging neckline, the small but perfectly formed breasts, the sparkling eyes combined with a receding chin. You can recognize the man by his dark tan, his muscled torso like that of a matador, the open shirt with the sexy, dark grizzly-bear hair on his chest. Yet both the men and the women tend toward being rather heavy later in life.

Sexually, this sign has a voracious appetite and can't seem to get enough. This can put a burden on a partner who is not as interested in sex. Taurus Rising is not necessarily promiscuous, because their planet-ruler Venus makes them want to "pair off" rather early in the relationship. This a slow-moving sign, however, and so is Taurus Rising's lovemaking. People born under Taurus Rising stay loyal lovers. They remain faithful and attentive and never lose their interest and curiosity about romance and sex. Older Taureans make some of the best lovers. Young Taureans are even better.

To Bed: Sing to Taureans in bed. Ask them about their favorite artist. Talk of music and then art. Top the evening off with a gourmet meal and a decadent dessert over candlelight. Do a bit of sexy slow dancing. Nuzzle Taurus Rising on the neck. Breathe hot and heavy in his ear. Don't go to bed right away. Taurus is a patient sign who appreciates not moving too fast into a sexual relationship or any other kind, for that matter. Be prepared that when you have sex, Taurus men are usually very well endowed. After all, there is no rush—at least, not for Taurus.

To Wed: Not rushing things? This is good because Taurus Rising is slow to make changes and this naturally includes marriage. If Taurus-Rising people had their way, they'd stay engaged for years. This is why it is good to bring up the idea of marriage or commitment rather gradually. It isn't necessarily that they don't want to commit; they just want to take it slow. Explain to your Taurus Rising that you are only making plans for both of your financial future. *This* is what Taurus Rising understands.

To Keep the Ego Fed: Remind Taurus Rising of what a great lover and an enduring lover he or she is.

What Taurus Rising Needs and Looks for in a Partner: Mystery, money, and emotional intensity is what Taurus Rising seeks in a partner. When we look at the natural polarity to Taurus, or the opposite sign of Taurus Rising, the astrological sign that fits the bill best is Scorpio. Taurus likes money and Scorpio likes making money. Both have strong sexual drives and hearty tastes. While Scorpio *believes* he is practical, Taurus Rising actually understands how to organize and pay the bills. Taurus and Scorpio are signs that aim high and usually hit their mark. For this reason, a person with the Sun or other planets in Scorpio is highly compatible with Taurus Rising.

GEMINI RISING

First, you will notice the bright, inquisitive eyes and the easy ability to laugh or make others laugh. Although Gemini Rising often seems easy to know, this sign is really rather complex. Geminis have minds that function on many levels. Gemini Rising talks a lot, often too much, but puts others at ease with his or her natural friendliness. People born under the Gemini Rising sign are usually quite popular and find it easy to strike up a relationship since they are never at a loss for words. Shy people love Geminis because they help others break out of their shells.

In short, Gemini finds most people and situations "interesting." This is why Geminis are abnormally smart and well versed in many areas. Their natural curiosity leads them in a number of fascinating directions; for this reason, they are teachers to the world.

Keep in mind that Gemini Rising is the least monogamous Rising sign of all, so if you feel yourself attracted to or involved with someone who was born when the Twins were rising, expect your partner to flirt, not only with you, but others who are "available" as well. In fact, this sign tends to delay marriage, thinking that he or she "might score better in the future." This is possibly their ugliest trait. They lack a certain loyalty to the people with whom they are most intimate. Or perhaps the real truth is that they are loyal to several different people and this causes all kinds of conflicts and contradictions in their lives.

Though fond of children, people with Gemini Rising often delay parenting or childbearing because, after all, they are children themselves who refuse to grow up. It is very difficult for a Gemini to give up his childhood or youth. Thus, their partners often become surrogate parents. Insecure people born with Gemini Rising tend to be attracted to authoritarian or bossy types because parental figures let them off the hook: they don't have to be adults.

As with most "kids," you can expect them to rebel every now and then. Put them with, say, a Pisces type, a person without direction or boundaries, and the whole damned relationship goes to hell in a handbasket. Irresponsible individuals make very poor partners for Gemini Rising, who is certainly smart but lacks a direction without being forced into one. Versatile and often artistically gifted, Gemini Rising tends not to finish projects and ends up drifting. The same is true of Gemini's romantic relationships, which often fizzle because of a lack of direction or excitement. The one quality Gemini can count on that will attract others is their youthful energy; they appear much younger than their biological age.

Living with Gemini-Rising people can be a challenge since they tend to be somewhat obsessive-compulsive individuals and are prone to bouts of insomnia. Their minds, though great, are much too active, which makes them unable to relax. Thus, they are prone to illnesses involving stress and anxiety. Strange, invasive thoughts and counting rituals are other reasons to worry. For this reason, Gemini Rising must stay constantly active so weird thoughts and worries don't drag him into a complete neurotic breakdown.

Gemini is not a hard sign to attract, as long as you appear thoughtful, intelligent, and willing to act silly and be a bit of a prankster. One way to keep this relationship going is to create the impression that you are much smarter, more sophisticated, or more creative than Gemini Rising. This works like a charm. Geminis are in awe of people whose minds surpass their own. This sign also admires humor and wit, so keep that in mind while dating. Show Gemini Rising that you can be a bit of a daredevil and are also independent. The thing that keeps Gemini around is your willingness to share and have fun.

To Bed: Wear short skirts or tight pants and don't be afraid to show your wit. Be willing to laugh, play hard, and dance the night away. Stay aware of popular culture. Learn about phone sex. Discuss sexual matters openly and honestly; Gemini Rising won't be embarrassed. This sign is endlessly curious about everything, including the latest sexual positions or games. Look at your love life as an adventure. Don't be afraid to be coy and "play games." Playing games with Gemini Rising is as natural as breathing air.

To Wed: Convince Gemini of your superior knowledge or ability to access information. Stay on top of the news and other intellectual matters. Stay on the cutting edge, intellectually. Give Gemini Rising a direction. Be a pal as much as a lover to Gemini. In order to become a "spouse" to a Gemini-influenced individual, you must also be his or her partner in "crimes of the heart," a confidante, a best friend. There is no other way. If you stay detached or disinterested in Gemini's hobbies and pursuits, this Rising sign will be gone in a heartbeat. Gemini Rising is a sign more *of the mind* than of the heart, body, or sex. Remember this always.

To Keep the Ego Fed: Compliment Gemini Rising on how quick and brilliant he or she is. Ask Gemini Rising whether he or she has ever thought about joining Mensa?

What Gemini Rising Needs and Looks for in a Partner: It may seem odd, but Gemini Rising looks for a partner who can give him freedom and distance without limits. Gemini individuals aren't necessarily looking for spouses or dependents. They're looking for someone to join them on their many adventures. Freedom-loving Sagittarius is the polarity sign to Gemini and governs the Seventh House of Partners for Gemini Rising. This Rising sign expects his or her partner to be a social animal, a lover who likes to gad about and circulate just as he does. The most compatible partner for Gemini Rising is a person born under the sign of Sagittarius or with planets such as Moon, Venus, or Mars in the fiery Archer sign.

CANCER RISING

Look for the shy smile and the averted gaze showing that Cancer-Rising people are a million miles away. Watch for the pale, dewy skin, the moist dreamy look in their eyes, and the moon-shaped round face. Let your Cancerian lover dream and hide. Understand his or her need to be private. This is the best way to first get romantic with Cancer Rising.

Cancer Rising is the most sympathetic sign, but those born under this sign can at first be unapproachable. They give the impression that they don't need company and want to be left alone. The real truth is, they have been wounded and are only trying to protect themselves from that happening again. Hypersensitive, Cancer Rising tends to be overly emotional, exaggerating past hurts as much more serious than they originally were. Their complaints are like works of art that they bring out to polish or embellish over and over again. Whatever unfortunate circumstance has happened to them is the worst thing that ever occurred—period!

Cancer Rising is one of the more introverted signs—which doesn't necessarily mean that all of them are shy; it just means they prefer to live in the world of their imaginations. They are "artists in their souls" but often end up in the helping professions. Cancer-Rising people have a natural affinity and great empathy for both children and the elderly. Their vast imaginations, however, can lead them into the fields of writing, bookmaking, or illustration.

Many make a great deal of money since Cancer Rising is the sign that naturally draws lucrative financial deals. (More millionaires are born under the sign of Cancer than any other sign.) Family and "roots" are *very* important. So if you end up romancing this sign, you'll have to listen to a lot of stories about family affairs or sometimes the tedious recounting of the grand old family tree. It's not unusual for Cancer to have been born into privilege or to a family that considers money or the making of it greatly important. As you get to know Cancer Rising, you'll notice that they tend to discuss how much money other people have. At least, the practical-minded Cancers do, whereas the others are spiritualists well above the vulgarity of the temporal world!

In romance, it takes a long time to win Cancer Rising's trust. You can expect to approach Cancerians more than once romantically before they start to respond; they are so very unsure and insecure. If Cancer Rising first approaches you, know that he or she is greatly attracted. Often Cancer Rising will send a friend over to break the ice. Like Virgo, Cancer is quite sensitive to rejection. (Actually, they expect to be rejected.) As romance ensues, Cancer is an incredibly responsive lover. After all, Cancer is the sign that governs touch, and Cancerian's breasts are their sensitive points. So when making love, if you fondle or kiss the breasts, it can bring Cancer to orgasm.

As a lover, Cancer Rising is responsive and sympathetic to your needs as long as his or her feelings and needs are considered. Cancerians are hesitant and often insecure about forming intimacies too quickly. In fact, they miss out on many important opportunities due to their hesitancy to form close alliances of all kinds. Cancer Rising can be a loner. When a close bond with Cancer is finally formed, however, it is rarely ever broken. Cancer Rising remains tied to his or her past. So if you're seriously involved with Cancer Rising, you can expect the affair to go on for a long time—perhaps forever.

To Bed: Cultivate intimacy and show that you can be trusted. Listen to the heartrending stories of Cancer Rising's childhood. Be sympathetic. *This* is very important. Touch him or her gently and frequently. Physical touch will finally win Cancer Rising over every time. Remember this.

To Wed: Never betray the trust of Cancer Rising. If you do, any physical relationship or serious plans or commitment will be shattered. Always be conscious of Cancer's feelings. An unintuitive or emotionally "tone-deaf" person is the wrong partner for Cancer Rising.

To Keep the Ego Fed: Compliment Cancer Rising on his or her exceptional ability to both remember and imagine. Begin to rely on Cancer Rising. People of this sign are helpers and find your confidence in them flattering.

What Cancer Rising Needs and Looks for in a Partner: The most healthy, satisfying relationship for a person with Cancer Rising to have is one based upon trust and stability. As a highly imaginative sign, Cancer isn't looking for fireworks and excitement so much as for peace and privacy. Capricorn is the polarity sign to Cancer and governs the Seventh House of Partners for individuals born with Cancer Rising. Someone with a Capricorn birthday, or a person with planets in Capricorn, is the most highly compatible and stabilizing partner for Cancer Rising.

LEO RISING

You can spot this Rising Sign by their proud strut and the dramatic toss of their hair. Like it or not, Leo Rising is a leader and attracts many followers, including stalkers and fanatical devotees. So, when you are romantically involved with a charismatic Leo Rising, you will have to share your lover with others. You will also have to stand in his or her shadow. Are you willing to do this?

There is no doubt about it: Leo Rising loves to shine. They love adoring crowds and appreciate being admired by many, sometimes more than they like sex one-on-one. After all, the power of fame and admiring minions is the biggest aphrodisiac of all. At least, that's how Leo Rising sees it. Since Leo Rising basks in the attention of others, he or she will always attract both publicity and gossip. Likewise, you will notice how people fight for this sign's attention.

Physically, this sign creates a dramatic, imposing appearance. Leo Rising is often taller than average, with perfect posture and a statuesque bearing. Even when they don't have the best-looking face or body in the crowd, they somehow manage to convince everyone that they do. After all, this is a vainglorious sign; common, everyday acts and functions are "beneath them." Thus, when involved in a romance with Leo Rising, as dazzling and passionate as it may become, you could easily end up their servant or slave. In fact, Leo-Rising people will help you feel special for being privileged just to serve them!

Then there is the part about how misunderstood and unappreciated they are, or how their superiority has been ignored.

People with Leo Rising will constantly remind you how special they are, how their genius is overlooked, or how their unique talents have been held back by the envy of others who oppose them at every corner. Listen to how incredibly great they are! Watch out—if you don't instantly agree or applaud, Leo will be gone in a solar flash!

Leo Rising is a passionate, usually dignified sign whose fragile ego is covered up by vainglorious attention-seeking antics that can be a real stomach-turner for people who appreciate a more modest approach. At his best, however, Leo Rising is an ennobling sign, able to supercede the needs of his ego to rise to some greater good. Leo works best for "a cause," but fame is his name and power is his game. Like Aries, Leo is primarily out for number one, and if you want to join the cause, he'll allow you to come along—just as long you don't stand in his spotlight or appear in any way, shape, or form more worthy of admiration than he is. Leo-Rising people can become very jealous of the attention bestowed upon their partners. (Prince Charles has Leo Rising—great for a king, but awful for the husband of an adorable Princess.)

As a lover, Leo Rising is pretty much the same: he is always on top and wants to be in the position of power. There is a funny thing about Leos. Many born under this Rising sign are so enamored of their own image that they will pick lovers or marry partners who resemble them. They are seldom are attracted to women who remind them of their mothers; they are attracted to women who remind them of themselves. Perhaps this is the closest Leos can come to making love to their own image in the mirror. Sexually, Leos make great lovers—not because of a powerful libido, but because they are performers and always aim to please their crowd, even if that crowd is only you.

In order to keep Leo Rising sexually or romantically interested, one good way is to mirror his or her appearance, manner of speaking, and gestures. You don't want to rebel against a Leo as you would a Sagittarius or a Gemini. Leo Rising would consider this a type of treachery and basically unforgivable. Instead, you should rebel with them, join them in their quest of doing things in a big and attention-seeking way. You can't go wrong in helping your Leo Rising keep all eyes fascinated and fixed *on him*.

To Bed: Leo needs flattery even more than affection. Pay close attention to this sign and never dismiss him or her. Give compliments freely and make sure you appear just as dramatic and attention-grabbing as Leo is. Stand with Leo Rising before a mirror and undress him slowly and deliciously—and don't forget about hanging that mirror above your bed!

To Wed: Let Leo Rising know that the opposite sex finds you quite "interesting" and you wouldn't lose much sleep if he wasn't around anymore. Make sure Leo knows that many other people want you. Make sure that he knows that winning your heart is every bit as good as winning an Academy Award.

To Keep the Ego Fed: This is both simple and complex. Compliments! Compliments! Compliments! Use some occasional restraint on the compliments, however, or else Leo Rising may get the idea he can do better and will venture off to look for a lover who is as impressive as Leo *thinks* he is.

What Leo Rising Needs and Looks for in a Partner: To unlock the secret of one sign's desires, you need only look at the opposite

sign, and for Leo Rising this sign is Aquarius. Leo Rising is looking for someone who is outrageously original. Like Leo,
Aquarius grabs attention, though not for the same reason! Leo Rising
loves attention just for the sake of having attention. Aquarius is just
eccentric. Put these two signs together and you have a legendary
pair. Thus, for Leo Rising, the most compatible partner would be
a person with an Aquarius birthday or natal planets in the Water-
Bearer sign.

VIRGO RISING

If your love interest has Virgo Rising, you're not dating a slouch.
You have just entered a relationship with a fastidious, intelligent,
and highly functioning human being. When you first meet Virgo
Rising, he or she may come across as shy, pensive, nervous, or
somehow lost in deep thought. The fact is, people with Virgo
Rising worry terribly, and when that worry has ended, another one
begins. Therapists call this an "obsessive-compulsive disorder."
Astrologers call this "the curse of having too much of a Virgo
influence in your horoscope."

Virgo Rising is in no rush to start a superficial relationship
or one that leads nowhere. They'd rather be alone, left to their
thoughts. A romantic sign, Virgo Rising is retiring and overly
sensitive. People are strangers until you get to know them and
that involves great emotional risk—something Virgo isn't too
fond of. To them, dating "friends of friends" is okay for the ten
years following graduation. After all, Virgo is in no rush, because
eventually that "perfect person" will come along. Virgo Rising

keeps waiting for the ideal partner, the soulmate who somehow never seems to show up. Therefore, Virgo will delay serious relationships for years in fear of making a mistake. Or Virgo Rising may think that a better, more perfect lover is the next one who is coming along.

This is why, in the past, you had the "Bachelor Virgo" or the "Old Maid Virgo." It isn't that they weren't sought after as lovers or partners. The simple fact is that very few lovers can make the grade for a person born with Virgo Rising. Virgos are perfectionists who analyze and criticize every small flaw that surfaces in potential partners. This type of fault-finding can poison even the best relationships.

Virgo-Rising people are also quite health-conscious. In fact, they are obsessed and spend a great deal of energy worrying about their health. Because Virgos are so worried about their health, they soon become talented at diagnosing their own health problems, as well as the health problems of others. Many people with Virgo Rising end up in the medical professions. Virgos also tend to be attracted to alternative medicines such as herbal remedies, vitamin therapy, and acupuncture. If you want to get the answer to a medical problem, seek the help of a Virgo. They can probably point you in the right direction to get assistance.

There are two types of Virgo Rising people—the highly organized, fastidious, vigilant, housekeeping Virgo who rations out every nickel and penny and the Sloppy Joe type. The latter dresses in cheap clothes, fills his pockets with artificial sweeteners when leaving restaurants, and drives an outdated piece of junk because "it's good enough" and Virgo doesn't want to spend the money on something he doesn't need (like dependable transportation). Women with Virgo Rising often fall between the puritanical "Church-Chat Lady" and Stevie Nicks' "Bohemian Witch." After all, this sign can be strange. Virgo-Rising people can be very fussy about health and diet, which is just another facet of their puritanical natures. It goes without saying that Virgo is a complex, multi-faceted sign.

Virgo Rising people are commonly workaholics and maintain conservative values. Early in their lives, Virgos have been taught to feel guilty over sex. It's not that Virgos can't enjoy sex—Virgo is actually one of the more sexual signs—it's just that sex is an area of shame for them, even more than for the general public. Sex addiction can become a problem for a few Virgos, in which the power of the taboo, which is sex, constantly looms over them, like a storm cloud, gaining power. Some of them eventually give up sex completely, but this is not common.

Most Virgos have a sweet sensitivity, and often their imaginations are as big as their need to organize. It's important that you not invalidate the Virgo Rising's worries as imagined or unreal. Virgo is sensitive to everything and must not be dismissed. Be sympathetic to Virgo Rising's occasional neuroses. Also, be thankful that you are with a partner who is sensitive to the needs of others. Allow Virgos to worry over and help tend to *your* problems. They like doing it.

To Bed: Maintain a squeaky-clean appearance and lifestyle. Appreciate convention and the status quo. Always remember that Virgo Rising tends to be repelled by sleazy things, bizarre sex rituals, or seedy interests. Unconventional sexual practices are about as attractive to Virgos as picking your nose in front of them. Don't do it!

To Wed: Never allow criticism to enter your relationship with Virgo Rising. You can be sure that Virgo will freely criticize; however, it's best that you nip this in the bud at the beginning of the relationship. Cultivate the compassion that is natural to Virgo. Be loyal in your relationship through the dark times. Stay strong and show that, like Virgo Rising, you have common sense.

To Keep the Ego Fed: Ego? Does shy Virgo have an ego? The answer is *yes*! Remind Virgo Risings how essential and *needed* they are. Remind Virgo Risings of their sexual attractiveness. Virgo-Rising people find this surprising but are pleased by it.

What Virgo Rising Needs and Looks for in a Partner: When we look at the polar opposite sign to Virgo Rising, we find sensitive and psychic Pisces. After all, Virgo Risings are highly sensitive and psychic, too, but just don't trust their abilities. Pisces has just the right brand of compassion and empathy that Virgo needs. Pisces, for better or worse, is also mutable and therefore a rather *free-living* sign, a healthy contrast to the sometimes poker-faced or strait-laced Virgo. Therefore, a Virgo-Rising person would find someone born under the sign of Pisces or having many planets in Pisces a most compatible partner or lover.

LIBRA RISING

This Rising sign is not hard to single out. Libra Rising is typically the best-looking person in the room! Women of this sign, like Elizabeth Taylor, are often quite glamorous. Yet even if those of this sign are not born glamorous, they dress in a dramatic and appealing way. After all, Libra Rising is the sign of sophistication and beauty.

Not only do they marry often, they usually have many, many love affairs. Promiscuous? Why, not at all! Libra Rising is in love with every person he or she happens to sleep with, whether it is for five minutes or five years. Ruled by Venus, Goddess of Love and Peace, men born with Libra Rising understand women better than any other Rising sign. This might sound odd because Libra is one of the masculine signs and has no trouble with assertiveness. However, Libra is charming and genteel. You hardly realize that he is asserting himself. Libra is always romantic and tends to put his lover on a pedestal, without being controlling in the way that Scorpio is.

The woman who ends up with a Libra-Rising man is lucky, because Libra understands how important it is to make a good appearance and is always aware of "feelings" and the need to communicate. Everyone refers to Libra Rising as "Such a lovely person." Libra is social, but not gregarious, and puts everyone at ease. People with this Rising sign are humanitarians but are cultivated in an artistic and intellectual way. Libra is the one who dreams up ways to help the needy but through a social platform, such as a benefit concert or an art auctions, rather than "hands on." (We cannot forget, however, that Libran Mother Teresa was about as "hands on" with the poor as one could get. She represents the highest example of Libra's humanitarian impulse.)

The appearance of Librans, as mentioned earlier, is normally quite attractive. While opposite sign Aries often has skin problems, Libra Rising has clear skin but with a certain ruddiness that looks healthy. The features of Libra-Rising people are quite uniform; even plain-looking people with Libra Rising rarely have one bad feature. The men have nice hair that is sometimes worn in an almost feminine style, while the women with Libra Rising are more "gussied up," with wigs, gemstones, fancy cosmetics, lashes, a cloud of perfume, and the latest styles. With all of these embellishments, however, Libra remains tasteful and is rarely tacky or "off the mark" when it comes to fashion, in the way that a Leo or Pisces can sometimes be.

Probably their most irritating trait is Libra Rising's tendency to "ride the fence" and never make a commitment or come to a decision. In other words, you'll have to do it for Libra. In fact, their inability to make a decision often ruins one of Libra's favorite things to do: *shop*. For Libra, shopping is a double-edged sword. Individuals born under this sign love to shop, will spend all day shopping, can't make up their minds, and will then buy something hastily as the store closes. So what happens later? Libra Rising is back at the store bright and early the next day to exchange the item bought in haste.

In romance, Libra Rising can be a rather codependent sign. People with Libra Rising want to be with someone, want to be married, want to be coupled, and it doesn't matter who their partner is. As popular and attractive as they are, they have trouble finding the ideal mate because they settle on just about anyone. Not wanting to "go it alone," Libra needs an ally, a soulmate, someone to reconcile the opposite sides of Libra's dual nature, which are always in conflict. When coupled, Libra is a devoted lover who remains social and charming and rarely ever strays.

To Bed: Communicate in the most charming way possible. Make sure you smell nice and look even better. Show an interest in culture. Strive toward being more sophisticated than the average person. Never talk dirty. Libra Rising hates smut and the people who spread it around. Make love as if you are in heaven, on clouds lined with silver, and near angels of gold playing musical lyres. Surround yourself with beauty. Beauty is the ultimate high to Libra Rising.

To Wed: Stay friends and share the same interests, working toward similar goals. Be with Libra Rising often. Pal around and discuss humanitarian issues. Once Libra Rising gets used to you being a great friend and a great lover, a stronger commitment will soon follow. Make sure it's a good match, for Libra loves to marry—often.

To Keep the Ego Fed: Remind Libra Rising how unusually attractive he or she is. Show confidence in Libra Rising's decisions. Libra agonizes over decisions. It goes without saying that your support is essential in keeping the relationship thriving.

What Libra Rising Needs and Looks for in a Partner: Libra is a mental sign, despite Libra Rising being very much the romantic and involved in "relationships." Libra Rising is really looking for passion and excitement. Libra's polar opposite is assertive Aries, long on excitement and short on patience. Opposite signs have both opposing and similar traits to each other. Libra and Aries are both rather ambitious signs.

While Libra Rising has charm and gentility, Aries has passion and zeal. They complement each other. Therefore, a person born with his or her Sun (and other planets) in Aries is the most compatible mate for Libra Rising.

SCORPIO RISING

Intense, puzzling, complicated, and intimidating—all of these words describe Scorpio Rising, the enigmatic sign of extremes. Individuals born under the sign of Scorpio are famous for their mystery, through perhaps the reputation of been a sexually driven sign is overrated. Scorpios hold feelings in and then mull them over for a long time. They are not a spontaneous sign, and this helps cultivate their sense of mystery.

Obviously, many Scorpios are spooky and we love them for it. Some are downright awesome—at least, they have tremendous psychic and psychological power. Scorpio Rising is the one sign you can actually *feel* enter a room. They have a deep, inner core that is impossible to reach. The truth is, Scorpio Rising can rarely reach the core level of his own being. He has tried to figure himself out for years and in the process has developed amazing inner resources and an understanding of human nature. Some people with Scorpio Rising become psychic detectives, mystery writers, or psychiatrists. Other Scorpios just stay, well, odd and detached. Scorpio Rising is the kind of person everyone gossips about, but no one really knows.

Some people with Scorpio Rising are loners and thus are hard to get close to or truly know. You will have to be patient with this sign, because knowing them and loving them is indeed worthwhile. They provide the most passionate romance and sex of all the Rising signs. They make great lovers and are quite tuned in to their partners, almost to a psychic degree.

Scorpio is ruled by both Mars and Pluto. Pluto was the god of the underworld; thus Scorpio is a sign associated with death as well as sex. Both experiences are a type of transformation. Sex is important to Scorpios because an orgasm is like what the French call a "little death." After all, Scorpio resembles the Egyptian god Osiris who recreates himself over and over. Scorpio, like Osiris, dies in the evening and is born anew in the morning with the Sun. For Scorpios, there are many deaths, in respect to life transitions. Often Scorpio will become deeply involved with groups and individuals for a while, then there is a "falling out" and Scorpio retreats back inside his desert cave, to transform, to rise above, to be born into a new life with new hopes and altered aspirations—and definitely *different* associations. These transformations are lifelong and quite intense and painful. Scorpio is a sign of the murdered and the murderer. It isn't easy being a Scorpio, but God, don't we love them?

When in a relationship with Scorpio Rising, expect to experience bizarre incidents of telepathy and all kinds of spooky, unexplained stuff. If you're into the "Goth" movement, well, it is Scorpionic to a T. Astrologer Alan Oaken writes that Scorpio is the sign of the Vampire, the charismatic Byronic hero, who "drains" his lover or "victim" with only enough energy left to be his slave. (Sorry, Scorpio, but you're so damned fascinating!)

A romance with Scorpio Rising can be trying. They make great emotional demands on the relationship and can be quite controlling. Scorpio is as famous for his lashing tongue as for his laser-like gaze. This sign will use cruel and cutting remarks to keep you in your place—that is, if you can catch him at it! Scorpio is underhanded, and it takes a while for the insult to sink in. Scorpio seldom fights directly. He fights under the covers, but he aims to win and usually does.

Scorpio Rising feels love or hate, the extremes of passion, and very little in-between. For Scorpio, sexual energy is divine and the lover the divinity. Enter a love affair or romance with Scorpio Rising with open eyes and with caution. Scorpio can take you to the heights of passion or into the bowels of hell. Scorpio Rising may very well be the greatest love of your life.

To Bed: This one is easy. The less clothes you wear, the more Scorpio will be driven crazy with desire—but avoid the lurid and sleazy. Scorpio wants you all to himself. "Flash" Scorpio discreetly—as if you don't realize you're doing it. Wear a backless dress, tight pants, or a skirt split up the side. Scorpio appreciates variation and sexiness to a degree that others do not. Be careful, though. I know of one couple in which the man with Scorpio Rising wanted his wife to leave her brunette wig on while they were making love. The marriage survived, but the wig didn't. It departed with the garbage the very next day.

To Wed: Allow Scorpio Rising to see that you understand him better than anyone, even better than he understands himself. Show that you are a person with certain resources and abilities, especially at making money. Scorpio is one of the "money signs." We tend to overlook this because we're so busy discussing Scorpio's sex life, or sex drive, or the lack of it. For Scorpio Risings to commit to a partner, they have to be sure the partner can carry his or her own weight financially. Some people feel that Scorpio is not romantic enough. Like Aries, Scorpio is too intensely involved in other issues, such as "Why am I here?" and "Why was I born?" After marrying this sign, expect intensity, build-ups, and breakdowns to be the normal routine.

To Keep the Ego Fed: Mention to Scorpio Rising what awesome power he or she has. Bring up Scorpio's mysterious beauty. Compliment Scorpio on his or her focus and ability to get things done.

What Scorpio Rising Needs and Looks for in a Partner: The polarity for Scorpio is the fixed sign Taurus. In trying to discover what Scorpio Rising truly must have in a romantic relationship, we need only look at the opposite sign of Taurus. Complicated and emotionally needy Scorpio seeks the loyalty and devotion that only a Taurus can give. Scorpio and Taurus are also quite sensual and would enjoy a great sex life. Therefore, Scorpio Rising would be most compatible with a person born under the sign of Taurus or someone who has a few planets in Taurus.

SAGITTARIUS RISING

Don't try to figure him out. This sign is an "open book." Sagittarius Rising doesn't keep secrets because he doesn't think the truth is anything to be ashamed about. He'll tell it like it is and he doesn't give a damn about what you think. Honesty is the best policy as far as Sagittarius is concerned. Believe it! Still, Sagittarius Rising will fill you in on all the ways you can improve yourself. After all, Sagittarius is an expert on many *philosophies* and he knows best.

If you want to have fun and love with wild abandonment, however, this sign is the one to go for. Sagittarius Rising is outspoken to the point of embarrassing to others. This person is smart and has many irons in the fire. With great creative zeal, Sagittarius goes after his ideals. The problem is, although Sagittarius Rising is quite spontaneous, his enthusiasm peters out the minute he hits a snag. Thus, many unfinished projects and plans lie scattered about his house. Look for lots of clutter, as well as an emotionally cluttered life.

Typically, people with Sagittarius Rising are somewhat larger than average. They have a tendency toward weight gain, but not in the bloated way of Cancer and Pisces, who tend heavily toward water retention. Ample hips and buttocks are a part of Sagittarius Rising's appearance. This sign has bright, clear eyes that sparkle and a broad, handsome face; however, there are diminutive Sagittarians who tend to be "elfin" in appearance, with childlike eyes forever twinkling with mischievously.

Romantically speaking, Sagittarius plays the field because he thinks he's supposed to. After all, Sagittarius is not the most romantic of signs. For Sagittarius, playing Romeo or Juliet is quite a stretch. People born under this Rising sign adore parties, lots of dancing, laughing, dirty jokes, and, at times, drinking. Ruled by jolly Jupiter, Sagittarius is the sign of excess. Whatever Sagittarius Rising gets, he just wants more of—this includes food, sex, alcoholic drinks, or husbands. This sign was born to play, not work— and that also means "playing around."

Sex with Sagittarius Rising is friendly and does the trick of bringing you to orgasm even though he or she is a little too fast at it. You have to constantly remind Sagittarius Rising of your feelings because, in most instances, this sign lacks empathy and can be emotionally tone-deaf. On a more positive note, Sagittarius Rising is optimistic, mostly positive, life-affirming, and eager to please his lover and get on to the next adventure. He is not a "detail person," so expect Sagittarius to gloss over everything, including other people's feelings and, of course, this also means yours. Learn to tell dirty jokes because Sagittarius Rising can be loud-mouthed and coarse.

While Libra Rising is "the marrying sign," Sagittarius Rising is "the bachelor sign." If you happen to see a seventy-year-old man driving a pepper-red sports car with a vanity license plate, you can pretty well assume this old guy has some Sagittarius in his horoscope. In keeping with this, Sagittarius Rising looks unbelievably young.

Sagittarius Rising is a sign that strives. Entering a relationship with this individual will bring you many adventures and experiences. Sagittarius is a traveler in mind and in body. At their best, people born under Sagittarius Rising have integrity and will fight for the truth no matter what the cost. As lovers, they are affectionate, silly, and playful and are always good for an impromptu roll in the hay. These clowns of the zodiac can see the "big picture" and are most passionate about their heartfelt and strangely twisted philosophies. As a romantic partner or love mate, Sagittarius is long on both friendship and affection. Let's put it this way—with Sagittarius Rising you will never grow cold!

To Bed: Skinny-dipping is a favorite activity of most Sagittarians, if they're in a place where they won't get caught. If you don't have access to a swimming pool, trying wrestling naked. That should do the trick. Sagittarius loves erotic struggles and sexy competitions. Stay as playful and open as possible. Talk philosophy, not love, and try not to get all mushy. Sagittarius Rising hates mushy situations almost as much as he hates hypocrites.

To Wed: Sagittarius Rising, as with most Sagittarians, is not a sign that wants to be married. It just isn't in their realm of thought and is rarely one of their goals. Sagittarians marry rather late. You know how it is when you start out to swim in the summer? You keep dipping your foot into the cold water, testing it and trying to get used to it, but you never do. Then you just take the plunge into the icy cold water, holding your breath, wondering if your heart will stop. Then it doesn't and you say to yourself, "Well, I guess it wasn't *that bad*." Commitment is just one of those things the Archer sign dreads. Some people dread tax audits. Sagittarius Rising dreads marriage, that's all.

To Keep the Ego Fed: Remember to ask Sagittarius Rising all kinds of philosophical questions. Listen to his or her criticism of politics and religion and respect his opinions. Opinions are very important to Sagittarius Rising.

What Sagittarius Rising Needs and Looks for in a Partner: Sagittarius Rising is searching for latitude and freedom in a relationship and no sign fits this bill any better than the Mercurial sign of Gemini. As the natural polarity to Sagittarius, Gemini is just as fun-loving and mischievous as the Archer sign. In looking at the opposite sign, we can also see what we lack. Thus, Gemini teaches Sagittarius Rising to be less opinionated and judgmental. For this reason, a person born under the sign of Gemini, or one who has a couple of planets in Gemini, would be a most compatible mate for Sagittarius Rising.

CAPRICORN RISING

Here we get down to the facts, the practical, the here and now, since Capricorn Rising is mostly a no-nonsense sign. Look for a slight stoop in their posture and an untiring mind focused on the bottom line, the real truth that he or she can see, hear, or feel. The attitude of Capricorn Rising is "Show me the money." This individual is strong and sure in heart and mind. They are usually fixed on one goal at a time. Capricorn Rising is usually not sympathetic to, nor does he understand, the imaginative and the speculative. Capricorn Rising appears very mature and serious in childhood. This Rising sign tends to look older and is sometimes larger in bone structure than other children of his age. Oddly, as Capricorns age they tend to look younger (except for the notorious prematurely gray hair, which usually is present when there is a great deal of Capricorn in the horoscope), growing more attractive and appealing upon reaching middle age.

Sexually, Capricorn Rising tends to be aloof because sex implies intimacy, and intimacy is what Capricorn avoids. This Rising sign still makes a talented lover, one of great endurance, as long as his or her trust is won—similar to Scorpio, but Capricorn isn't under the yoke of sex as much as a Scorpio. It does not control him. At the same time, if you're into "feelings" and "sharing," this creates a conflict. Capricorn Rising does not like sharing his feelings because he doesn't know where they are; he's buried them for so long. Thus, Capricorn makes up feelings, and pretends to share emotions in order to further the relationship, which only makes the gap larger. Getting in touch with Capricorn Rising's feelings is a bit like being a doctor or a midwife helping a woman give birth. You have to softly slide your hands inside and then gently ease their feelings out. This is hard to do when it comes to Capricorn Rising. You can't force Capricorn. If so, there will be trauma. This Earth-bound Rising sign will instantly shut down and you'll never get another peek at that austere, chilly wasteland of emotions again.

Capricorn Rising typically controls his feelings and is generally skeptical or cynical about frail human emotions. Discipline and common sense mean everything to Capricorn. Practical issues are of great importance when it comes to commitment or marriage. This sign, more than the others, tends to marry for money, position, or prestige, as opposed to love, and generally, this is the way it stays. Because of money or status, Capricorn Rising will not divorce. Therefore, if you are involved with Capricorn Rising, understand that practical matters, such as your potential for making money in the future or the status of your family, may well take precedence over sentiment. Rarely is Capricorn Rising driven by passions. In fact, you could even say he is blind to passion. This Rising sign is primarily looking for a meal ticket or a way to find one. There are exceptions, of course, but only if there is a great deal of Fire or Water in the chart.

Generally, Capricorn Rising is always preparing for the "high life," in which he can gaze down at the miserable unfortunates from his mountainside perch. After all, Capricorn is the most ambitious of signs, and this means in all matters, including romance. Therefore, this sign tends to pursue the most desirable person (at least, in the eyes of others) or someone who is rich or privileged and can help Capricorn along in his search for high social status. If Capricorn understands any issues well, they would be social attitudes, conventions, and institutions.

Basically, Capricorn Rising wishes to hook up with people in power. This might be a clique, a group, a church, a university, or the U.S. government. So if you have success written all over you, Capricorn Rising will certainly be behind you all the way to the bank. If you are indolent or lazy, though (and who would ever admit this?), there could be a few problems. Hell for an unmotivated, lazy person would be a life married to a Capricorn. Conversely, it would be Heaven to be married to a Capricorn Rising who has worked hard and attained many of his cherished goals. After all, with Saturn, the planet of law and truth, as his guide, Capricorn can be the greatest of teachers. He is a truth-seeker who has nothing to hide.

To Bed: Not so easy, as Capricorn generally does not like to get close too fast. If he does want sex fast, this is a very bad sign because it means he has no intention of getting emotionally intimate with you and has no designs on you for the future. The best way to get intimate is over a glass of wine while each of you defines your own goals. Capricorn is attracted to and admires people with ambition.

To Wed: Show Capricorn you have control over your own goals and your own life. Show him that you are sympathetic and also have common sense. Be realistic and cautious in your approach, and, most of all, be a success at what you do. Don't cling or lean in the beginning of the relationship. Show Capricorn that you are a person who has resources.

To Keep the Ego Fed: Stand firmly behind Capricorn Rising in his or her ambitions and lofty pursuits. Never mention to a Capricorn that a goal is too high or a plan for success is too far-fetched. Once their minds are made up, no one can stop Capricorns from reaching their goals.

What Capricorn Rising Needs and Looks for in a Partner: As the polarity to Capricorn, Cancer is extremely resourceful and strong. Each sign requires stability in a partner, although not for the same reasons. Cancer is an emotionally insecure sign, while Capricorns pride themselves in having good old common sense, often at the expense of denying emotional needs. The truth is, both signs are rather complex and needy. Yet Cancer, being protective of home, family, and possessions, is a good match for the sign of the Goat. Therefore, anyone with a Cancerian birthday or who has a couple of planets in Cancer makes an ideal mate for Capricorn Rising.

AQUARIUS RISING

People who are born when Aquarius is Rising usually have a style of dress or expression of personality that is unusual or unique—although, unlike Leo in his need to be "vainglorious" and the center of attention at all times, Aquarius Rising is just odd. This Rising sign is averse to being like other people because the status quo seems dull and boring. You must keep in kind that Aquarius Rising is a "mental sign." Ideas and ways of doing things tend to get old or tired rather quickly.

Although they are "joiners" to certain "groups" or "cliques," Aquarius-Rising people are still very much aware of their own individuality. Admittedly, the groups Aquarius usually connects with are on the fringe, like Ghost Hunters Anonymous, UFO clubs, computer geek networks, Wiccans and Neo Pagans, and often those re-enacting Sword and Sorcery organizations. In other words, Aquarius Rising enjoys being the strangest among the odd. What could be more fun?

It goes without saying that Aquarius Rising has great vision. This sign sees waves of the future clearer than any other sign. Often, this sign has fashion and technological ESP. Usually what is obvious to Aquarius now, such as a social craze or fashion rage, will simply be how things will look to the rest of us two to five years down the road. If you want to follow trends, just follow Aquarius Rising around for a while. You'll pick up on something that will be turn out to be "hot" later. In this way, Aquarians are truly amazing.

Sexually, people with this Rising sign remain unconventional, but it's important not to paint them with a broad brush. As teenagers, they bring home whatever upsets their parents. Later, their romantic attractions tend to get more extreme, but they learn to hide it. Whatever is the norm in Aquarius in childhood is generally *not* what he seeks in a lover.

Bisexuality is a common Aquarian theme. Of course, this doesn't mean all Aquarians are gay. But Aquarius Rising gravitates toward the unfamiliar and certainly the unconventional, and this often includes bisexual affairs. After all, Aquarius is the sign of brotherhood and sisterhood, so all are included. It makes little difference that a person is of the same sex. They're human, aren't they? That means they're A-okay with Aquarius.

Aquarius-Rising people reject whatever they were raised around as children. Many Aquarians associate their childhoods with boredom and repression. In this way, they are not free to "sex" who they want to "sex." Later they strike out on their own, looking for forbidden territory as well as variety and strangeness in sexual partners. An Aquarian's partner may be a person of a different race or ethnic background, or a lover who belongs to a rather strange religious cult. The personality type that Aquarians are the most attracted to, however, would be the artists and anarchists of our culture, individuals who tend to "tweak" conventional people out of the coma of their mundane existence, much in the way that Aquarius does.

Aquarius Rising people are high-strung and have an overactive nervous system. This is the sign of electricity; thus you can see an electrical quality to their personalities as they smile and circulate around the room. Aquarius can be flighty and rather fanatical about what they choose to believe in. As lovers, they like to experiment and play roles during lovemaking. Aquarius Rising will show you worlds you only dreamed of. Learn to appreciate the unusual and experimental. Allow your romance with Aquarius to be truly electrifying.

To Bed: Your first approach should be unusual, either in manner of dress or in the way you express yourself. A "trans-gender" sense of style is charismatic to many, and this is even more true when it comes to the sign Aquarius Rising. Also, uniforms are quite attractive to the Water-Bearer sign, especially when the outfit has a sci-fi flair like the clothing for a *Star Trek* movie or something from the *X-Files*. Always remember that, in general, Aquarius looks up to the weird and different, so be certain to show Aquarius that you're the strangest person in the room.

To Wed: Aquarius is not usually someone who goes nuts over the idea of marriage. Aquarians are dispassionate, preferring friends and pals over romance. As long as you realize that Aquarius is not romantic in an old-fashioned way, the less you will be disappointed. If you look at this in a more positive light, however, you will see that it's much better this way. Friends make the best lovers. Friends also make the best marriage partners. By the time you become Aquarius Rising's *best friend*, you can be assured that marriage or commitment will soon follow. Stay with Aquarius. Be a friend.

To Keep the Ego Fed: Aquarians need to feel special, and that means *different* from everyone else. Compliment Aquarius Rising on his or her originality and genius. Aquarius does not wish to be one among the ordinary. Remind Aquarius of his or her potential for greatness.

What Aquarius Looks for and Needs in a Partner: As the polarity to Aquarius, Leo is a sign of drama and great emotional warmth. These traits are often lacking in Aquarius, who is nevertheless quite social and friendly. There is a big pay-off to each of these signs if they decide to move into the realm of romance and partnerships. Because Aquarians are unusual, they tend to attract attention and fascinate, which Leo loves. On the other hand, Leo is popular and admired, which Aquarius rather likes. For Aquarius Rising, a partner with a Leo birthday or a couple of planets in Leo is the perfect match.

PISCES RISING

As a sign that someone has Pisces Rising, look for softness and gentleness in the features. Look for womanly, pillow lips (Elvis had a Pisces Moon) and dreamy, unsure eyes. This super-sensitive Rising sign can be a pushover, a slave to love, or a victim. After all, Pisces has so few boundaries. Whether your lover is a male or female, you will have to be quite aware at all times of the vulnerable, emotional nature of this sign. You should not criticize Pisces-Rising people too harshly. They are psychic, intuitive, instinctive, living in a world of sensation and flow, an atmosphere of mood and emotions. Pisces Rising senses disapproval. No words are needed.

Pisces Rising has a quiet strength that fascinates. Individuals born under this Rising sign are compelling and have charisma, but few appreciate their own inner resources. So few of this sea-swept Rising sign can truly appreciate their own worth. They are so empathic, they do not know where they end and other people begin. Pisces is the sign of consciousness. After all, Pisces are the ocean that is the source of all life. They are the beginning and they are the end. The sign of Pisces is the sign of *continuance*.

Physically, Pisces Rising comes in two types—the large and the small. The larger Pisceans tend to retain a great deal of fluid; therefore, their bodies are not solid and the fat seems to float. Their features are soft and their appearance is generally quite vulnerable, with child-sized hands and feet. Keep in mind that Pisces Rising can be a very beautiful sign, quite compelling in appearance. Often, this Rising sign produces good looks but with some extra weight. On the other hand, the small, highly nervous Pisces is another common type. These Pisceans tend to remain small because they worry, worry, worry; do not eat; and are hypersensitive. The heavy Piscean type is extremely sensitive as well, but people of this type console themselves with food.

Sexually, Pisces Rising is complicated. People born under this sign are uncertain of their ability to attract or satisfy another person sexually. Pisceans tend to go for partners who have some serious dysfunction, disability, or character flaw. Thus, they become involved with persons having substance abuse problems, people who break the law, or those who are somehow abusive, directly or indirectly. Pisces Rising thinks, "I know I am being hurt—but who is hurting me?" Often, it is the person that Pisces feels closest to. The most romantic feelings a Piscean has exist long before the romance is in full swing. The thought of the lover, or love object, stimulates feelings of romance in Pisces Rising's imagination. It isn't necessary that the actual person be present.

The actual living person often ends up a huge disappointment to Pisces Rising—not because he is any different than he has ever been. Pisces just refuses to see the clues that are in plain sight. This is why Pisces often experiences heartbreak and unrequited love. Pisces Rising is all too willing to worship at the feet of his or her beloved as an indolent slave, dreaming of sexual adoration, rather than be an equal.

In terms of romance, Pisces Rising is the most romantic sign of all for this individual would surely die for love. Unfortunately, many do, by sacrificing themselves to a dual god of fantasy and passion. Treat Pisces-Rising people gently, for these most devoted of lovers deserve to have their dreams affirmed and their fantasies made real.

To Bed: Pisces is the sign of the feet, and individuals with Pisces Rising are quite enamored of beautiful legs and feet and a great pair of shoes. Pisceans are also fascinated with costuming, such as capes, boots, wigs, and clothing that evoke a sense of romance. If you wear your fantasies on your sleeve, this will sexually stimulate Pisceans. They'll aim to have you in bed quickly. Just remember "the look" you must bring across—like a character out of an

TABLE OF RISING SIGNS

SUN SIGNS

	Aries	Taurus	Gemini	Cancer	Leo	Virgo
4 A.M.–6 A.M.	Aries	Taurus	Gemini	Cancer	Leo	Virgo
2 A.M.–4 A.M.	Pisces	Aries	Taurus	Gemini	Cancer	Leo
Midnight–2 A.M.	Aquarius	Pisces	Aries	Taurus	Gemini	Cancer
10 P.M.–Midnight	Capricorn	Aquarius	Pisces	Aries	Taurus	Gemini
8 P.M.–10 P.M.	Sagittarius	Capricorn	Aquarius	Pisces	Aries	Taurus
6 P.M.–8 P.M.	Scorpio	Sagittarius	Capricorn	Aquarius	Pisces	Aries
4 P.M.–6 P.M.	Libra	Scorpio	Sagittarius	Capricorn	Aquarius	Pisces
2 P.M.–4 P.M.	Virgo	Libra	Scorpio	Sagittarius	Capricorn	Aquarius
Noon–2 P.M.	Leo	Virgo	Libra	Scorpio	Sagittarius	Capricorn
10 A.M.–Noon	Cancer	Leo	Virgo	Libra	Scorpio	Sagittarius
8 A.M.–10 A.M.	Gemini	Cancer	Leo	Virgo	Libra	Scorpio
6 A.M.–8 A.M.	Taurus	Gemini	Cancer	Leo	Virgo	Libra

Anne Rice novel, a bit romantic and gothic. For Pisces, the imagination rules! Be a person who is fantasy-driven. Pisces Rising will
be hot for you in no time.

To Wed: Remain the kind of lover Pisces Rising dreams of. Show
that you can make decisions and that you have a strong direction.
Pisces Rising lacks direction and is greatly attached to people with
confidence. Never be afraid to lead or direct people with Pisces
Rising. Actually, Pisceans like being bossed; they find it comforting.

To Keep the Ego Fed: Mention Pisces Rising's mysterious
charisma often. Support Pisces in all of his creative ventures.
Remind Pisces Rising of what a great artist he or she can be.

TABLE OF RISING SIGNS

SUN SIGNS

	Libra	Scorpio	Sagittarius	Capricorn	Aquarius	Pisces
4 A.M.–6 A.M.	Libra	Scorpio	Sagittarius	Capricorn	Aquarius	Pisces
2 A.M.–4 A.M.	Virgo	Libra	Scorpio	Sagittarius	Capricorn	Aquarius
Midnight–2 A.M.	Leo	Virgo	Libra	Scorpio	Sagittarius	Capricorn
10 P.M.–Midnight	Cancer	Leo	Virgo	Libra	Scorpio	Sagittarius
8 P.M.–10 P.M.	Gemini	Cancer	Leo	Virgo	Libra	Scorpio
6 P.M.–8 P.M.	Taurus	Gemini	Cancer	Leo	Virgo	Libra
4 P.M.–6 P.M.	Aries	Taurus	Gemini	Cancer	Leo	Virgo
2 P.M.–4 P.M.	Pisces	Aries	Taurus	Gemini	Cancer	Leo
Noon–2 P.M.	Aquarius	Pisces	Aries	Taurus	Gemini	Cancer
10 A.M.–Noon	Capricorn	Aquarius	Pisces	Aries	Taurus	Gemini
8 A.M.–10 A.M.	Sagittarius	Capricorn	Aquarius	Pisces	Aries	Taurus
6 A.M.–8 A.M.	Scorpio	Sagittarius	Capricorn	Aquarius	Pisces	Aries

What Pisces Rising Looks for and Needs in a Partner: Individuals born under the sign of Pisces Rising need a lover who can help them define themselves. Partners who can teach Pisces-Rising people about rules and boundaries are essential in helping them to stay on the right path—one that is clear and uncluttered. As polar opposite to Pisces, the sign Virgo exemplifies the qualities Pisces needs; they stay organized and stick with their goals, yet remain supportive and loving in their approach. Virgo and Pisces are equally sensitive, and, in some respects, they both worry too much. If your lover has Pisces Rising, look for Virgo influences in your own chart, such as your Sun sign or other planets in Virgo.

While the Rising sign and the Seventh House Cusp are keys to finding a romance that endures and turns into marriage, there are other factors indicating compatibility in a horoscope. If you don't find any connections between your chart and that of your lover's when reading the previous descriptions, horoscopes contain other factors that suggest sexual and romantic compatibility. One would be if your lover has a couple of planets in the same sign as your Rising sign (also know as the Ascendant) and vice versa. Another factor would be if you and your lover share many of the same elements, such as signs in Fire and Water, or Air and Earth. The most important way to make love work astrologically would be to read up on your lover and attempt to understand the style or tone of his or her horoscope as well as your own. Learning about yourself and your lover, planet-wise, can only lead to deeper empathy between you. This in turn leads to a deeper commitment. After all, it is written in the stars.

SEVEN

WRITTEN IN THE STARS: DESTINY, ROMANCE, AND SATURN SIGNS

Saturn is the planet that scares the hell out of astrologers. After all, Saturn stands for suffering, but even more important, for correction and the truth. The only time one needs to be afraid of Saturn is when one is afraid of the truth. Everyone has a Saturn sign, even though we may wish we didn't. Saturn brings much toil and effort.

In essence, Saturn is also the planet of limitations and paying one's dues. In astrology, Saturn lords over destiny, fate, and that over-used Eastern concept of karma in the horoscope. The word *karma* simply means that you get back whatever you have given, either in this lifetime or another. This is why Saturn is so important in looking at romance, marriage, and fated love affairs in your birth chart or your lover's. Since Saturn usually stays in a sign for more than two and a half years, Saturn can represent not only our peers and the people we go to school with, but also whom we choose to love and why.

Typically, some of our strongest attractions and most passionate love affairs involve aspects with the rainbow-colored,
ringed planet. In looking at close karmic (destined) love affairs,
one need not look much further than Saturn. Usually when there
is a strong attraction that leads to commitment, the planet Saturn
is involved. For instance, if the charts of two married people do
not have strong or beneficial Saturn aspects between them, the
marriage usually will not survive. There is simply not enough substance to the relationship.

When comparing the charts of two people who are happily in love, or just mildly attracted, you can expect to find
some Saturn connections. By Saturn connections, I simply mean
that when Saturn is in a sign in your chart, such as Leo, you
can expect to find planets in your lover's chart in Leo and possibly the Rising sign in Leo. You can take this a step more and
look for Fire signs in your lover's chart. Opposing signs
(Aquarius is Leo's opposing sign) also imply karmic connections. If any of these signs connect, then there is a natural
Saturn (destined) connection.

Not only does the planet Saturn represent the past in
terms of our childhood, the ringed planet also represents past
lives and who we are destined to be with in this present lifetime. Saturn stands for the measure of time and what we choose
to do with our lives. Saturn also implies the lovers we are fated to
meet and be with.

Do you and your lover have a Saturn connection? Look at
your Sun, Moon, Venus, Mars, and Rising signs. Look at your
lover's natal Saturn and vice versa. Turn the charts around and
study them closer. Can you read and understand the karmic connection? Read on and find out how your destinies connect.

SATURN IN ARIES

For those born from January 1938 through March 1940 or March 1967 through April 1969 or April 1996 through June 1998. Individuals with Saturn in Aries tend to isolate themselves, but once they are involved romantically they have great difficulty in letting go when the affair ends. There is a strong element of independence to this sign, but also a great deal of emotional self-torture. After all, Aries feels passion but Saturn freezes that passion. Thus, when in the sign of Aries, Saturn is in its detriment. This individual does not feel at all secure, especially when it comes to love and sex. Saturn-in-Aries people are known to be loners and are quite misunderstood by others. Aries wants to be self-sufficient and spontaneous, but Saturn still casts its gloomy cloud, making this individual unable to act in a free and open manner. This causes Saturn-in-Aries individuals to seem brooding, brutish, and punitive toward lovers. This is a greatly ambitious sign, since Aries wants to be Number One and Saturn wishes to rule the material world. This is strong lover who is often misunderstood.

If Your Lover's Saturn in Aries Connects With Your Sun, Moon, Venus, Mars, or Rising Sign: In past lives, you were war buddies together, united in spirit and soul, working toward one cause. Both of you are survivors in this life (as well as others), and this brings you even closer as you compare battle scars and emotional wounds. You work best when you are working together as a team of two, but no more. Saturn in Aries demands loyalty and you are willing to give it. Understand that Saturn in Aries calls all of the shots. Also understand that you must take a stand and can't back down, in order to make this relationship work. Your past life connections and your lover's are to one of the warrior groups such as the Vikings, Plains Indians, or ancient Romans.

SATURN IN TAURUS

For those born from April 1940 through May 1942 or May 1969 through June 1971 or July 1998 through August 2000. This is probably one of the more materialistic placements of Saturn because, for Saturn-in-Taurus people to feel secure, they must own lots of things, including trinkets, degrees, awards, accolades, and also lovers, the prettier or more handsome, the better. Individuals with Saturn in Taurus are in love with whatever it is they want to own. People with this Saturn sign can be lecherous and covetous at times, while at other times they are the most open and generous people on the face of the planet. Sex is a place of great inhibition and stress for them, even though they are famous for loving sex. People with Saturn in Taurus desire to own and control the person they make love to. "All mine!" roars Saturn in Taurus. These individuals are quite lusty, but they tend to feel guilty about it. They are prone to feelings of guilt and blame and to illicit affairs. They are also sexually charismatic.

If Your Lover's Saturn in Taurus Connects With Your Sun, Moon, Venus, Mars, or Rising Sign: In past lives, you lived in the lap of luxury with your lover, placated by material objects and various sensual pleasures. Your relationship now, as in the past, is an enormous power struggle in which you and your lover go through cycles of domination and submission. You look to the one with Saturn in Taurus to take the reins and lord it over you, yet all the while you resist complete domination. In many ways, your relationship is like that of a parent and child. Your common goal in love is to work toward building something of strong beauty and influence, or something that makes life easier for others. In past lives, you and your lover experienced wealth. If you play your cards right, in this life you will enjoy the same. Your past life connections and your lover's may have been in very early ancient Egypt, among the Druids, during Elizabethan times in Europe, or in China.

SATURN IN GEMINI

For those born from June 1942 through June 1944 or March 1972 through July 1973 or September 2000 through August 2002. The ultimate chameleon, this Saturn sign tends to show the face that others want to see. Saturn-in-Gemini people are versatile and slippery, most especially when it comes to love affairs. They are also shamefully flirtatious to people of both sexes. Even so, Saturn-in-Gemini people worry about communications, how they communicate with others, whether they are being lied to, or whether they are lying themselves. Where Saturn is, expect fear and anxiety to lurk there. Woe to the writers, journalists, or teachers born with Saturn in Gemini, as they must work harder than most; however, they usually end up more successful than the rest, because, after all, Saturn does not represent easy gains. Rewards gleaned in the Saturn placement of your chart point to substantial wins, only accomplished through forceful effort. Saturn in Gemini relates to words and can imply greatness, especially with speeches. Saturn in Gemini can point out bisexuality or the courting of more than one lover at a time. This sign is mercurial and curious but still feels very confined.

If Your Lover's Saturn in Gemini Connects With Your Sun, Moon, Venus, Mars, or Rising Sign: Language between you and your lover is an area of some difficulty. It may be that your lover doesn't trust or approve of what you have to say. A situation may develop where complete honesty is not encouraged or cultivated. In past lives, you traveled with your lover on many different adventures, across foreign or exotic lands. In those lives, you were friends before lovers; consequently, this area should be developed in the present life. In this way, friendship will be the bridge to a true and committed romance. Areas where you and your lover spent past lives together were places like ancient Greece, the Italian countryside, North Africa, and France.

SATURN IN CANCER

For those born from June 1915 through June 1917 or June 1944 through August 1946 or August 1973 through September 1975. Individuals born with Saturn in Cancer are typically quite introverted and prone to fits of melancholy. Depression always seems to be a factor in their lives, not so much because they tend to live depressing lives, but because they choose to dwell upon an unhappy past or other regrets. The Saturn-in-Cancer person needs privacy in order to recover from emotional losses and love affairs. Very often the most loyal of lovers, Saturn-in-Cancer individuals are devoted to those they choose to love, and their love affairs tend to be long-lasting. Part of this stems from the fact that Saturn in Cancer hates change of any kind and has trouble moving forward. People with this complex Saturn sign are too busy recalling how loved ones in the distant (and not so distant) past have wronged them. Saturn-in-Cancer persons need help with fluctuating moods and depressions. After some prodding, talking things out works best for them. Be willing to mull over their pasts, with a gentle reminder for them to move upward and onward, acknowledging their losses bittersweetly and yet letting go of those losses, as well.

If Your Lover's Saturn in Cancer Connects With Your Sun, Moon, Venus, Mars, or Rising Sign: Note that this is a highly emotional connection, and the karmic connections are indeed strong ones. Expect this relationship to hurt a little. Your lover may be preoccupied with someone in his or her past, who in reality probably meant very little but has now become an icon in his or her imagination but certainly not in fact. After all, Saturn in Cancer imagines very well. This is why it is so easy for this sign to become depressed. Early emotional wounds are remembered and reimagined as deeper than they actually were. Your past life connections with your lover may have been in a number of places, but primarily in Africa, among the Celts in Scotland, Ireland, or France, and in early America. It is even probable that in those past lives you and your lover worked together with various forms of magic. Saturn in Cancer is psychically powerful.

SATURN IN LEO

For those born from July 1917 through August 1919 or August 1946 through October 1948 or June 1976 through July 1978. Saturn restricts the natural openness of Leo, and, therefore, this placement indicates individuals who are fearful of outsiders. They generally have trouble sharing themselves and their world with people they don't somehow feel a connection to. To be sure, this sign, along with the other Leo signs, yearns to be famous and admired. The devotion of many is the only way Saturn in Leo feels secure. One can just imagination how insecure Leo feels in the most emotionally vulnerable area of love affairs. Others must stay at a distance while Saturn in Leo performs for his own in-group or clique. Don't expect to be invited to get closer if you're not in the clique, as Saturn in Leo is quite suspicious. Another curiosity about Saturn-in-Leo individuals is they put off having children. This is because they see themselves as kids and don't want the competition of having others around. Saturn in Leo wants his lover to admire him alone and tends to be jealous of any attention bestowed on a lover or another in his crowd.

If Your Lover's Saturn in Leo Connects With Your Sun, Moon, Venus, Mars, or Rising Sign: Saturn in Leo wants you to be his audience and he also wants you all to himself. Although people with this sign yearn for attention, as most Leo signs do, they tend to be restricted. Someone called them a name or told them to stop showing off as children and now they are afraid of public humiliation. Saturn in Leo fears that attention will only bring criticism or ridicule. In past lives, you and your lover were connected through your fame or royalty in various influential cultures such as the Aztec people and other related Meso-American nations, at the height of ancient Egyptian culture, and through African cultures, or during the time of the French Revolution.

SATURN IN VIRGO

For those born from September 1919 through September 1921 or October 1948 through December 1950 or August 1978 through September 1980. This sign worries and obsesses a great deal. Individuals with Saturn in Virgo tend to torture themselves (and others) over the small things that go wrong. Saturn in Virgo's world must be nearly perfect—a world in which lovers aren't about to make mistakes. Saturn in Virgo expects no less. Needless to say, this puts great strain on lovers and families. Individuals born under this Saturn sign also worry inordinately about germs and illnesses. In fact, they are quite talented when it comes to health matters and many end up in the helping or medical professions. More than any other Saturn sign, this sign strives for order and flawlessness. They make great book editors and accountants and excel in any profession where they strive toward a high standard of excellence. Saturn-in-Virgo individuals don't mind serving lovers, but in return they require loyalty and sometimes servitude from their lovers. These individuals are born with high-functioning minds and intellects, but they are restricted by their demand for perfection in all things, no matter how trivial.

If Your Lover's Saturn in Virgo Connects With Your Sun, Moon, Venus, Mars, or Rising Sign: The Saturn-in-Virgo person seeks peace and calm in relationships. Emotional closeness and protection usually means more than sexual passion. In romance, Saturn in Virgo is quite dedicated unless betrayed. Then this sign can completely turn against you. Saturn in Virgo is rather conservative in all areas and demands order and predictability when it comes to sex. Saturn in Virgo tends to be repressed and sometimes "acts out" sexually in strange or bizarre ways. In past lives, Saturn in Virgo was either miserly or was the victim of a tyrannical political system. It is possible that in a past life you and your lover were made to suffer because of your love for each other. Areas of past lives may have been early China, or other Asian countries, as well as in the ancient societies of Assyria, Sumeria, and Mesopotamia.

SATURN IN LIBRA

For those born from October 1921 through 1923 or August 1951 through October 1953 or October 1980 through November 1982. With this position, romantic relationships, unfortunately, are areas of suffering. Saturn-in-Libra individuals tend to marry either too young, foolishly, or never at all. Individuals with Saturn in Libra feel great anxiety and many doubts when it comes to romance and sexual affairs. They dread being alone, and yet this is precisely what happens, because often their standards are either too high or too unusual to find the perfect mate. People with this sign are always in the process of circulating, among friends, lovers, and groups. They want to fix you up and cure you of your loneliness since they aren't able to cure themselves of the same affliction. Those with Saturn in Libra are often free-wheeling gypsies living out of a suitcase between their many adventures with their blessed "connections." As with other Libra signs, this placement believes that somehow the perfect affair, romance, or marriage will lead to ultimate fulfillment, so this is the script they keep playing at over and again, until they, and everyone else, are too damned old to care. Be patient, as this sign is very helpful and kind to others.

If Your Lover's Saturn in Libra Connects With Your Sun, Moon, Venus, Mars, or Rising Sign: As long as you are willing to live the gypsy life, one of adventure and romance, Saturn in Libra is the ideal partner. This sign is desperate for the perfect romance but tends to get cold feet when it comes to marriage. After all, Saturn-in-Libra individuals don't want to do anything to break the spell of romance they have cast. They're not into real-ism and this is probably one of the reasons they get hurt easily. In past lives, you and your lover were partners who worked or conspired together. You had associations with both royalty and government. At that time, you and your lover were most likely close friends of the same sex. Possible areas of past lives were Indochina, Germany, Denmark, and parts of Eastern Europe among the Gypsies.

SATURN IN SCORPIO

For those born from September 1924 through November 1926 or November 1953 through January 1956 or September 1983 through November 1985. Sensitive and afraid of losing their powers, those with Saturn in Scorpio are often quite controlling in their romantic affairs and relationships. Saturn in Scorpio wants to own your mind, body, and soul and nothing less! Because these individuals are so deeply passionate and also psychic, they radiate tons of charisma, and so are never left without a lover for very long. Saturn in Scorpio forms deep and lasting attachments, unless you have fallen out of their favor, and then you might as well be dead: Saturn in Scorpio will never speak to you again. There is nothing superficial about a Scorpio, and this is especially true of Saturn in Scorpio, who takes everything to heart. Cool and somewhat remote on the outside, Saturn in Scorpio often has buried hostilities left over from childhood. It's likely Saturn in Scorpio's parents didn't get along very well, and this makes him fearful of marriage. This sign is also prone to rage, paranoia, or resentment. While charismatic to the maximum level, this sign remains rather closed, secretive, and guarded. They are also very protective of their own affections and interests.

If Your Lover's Saturn in Scorpio Connects With Your Sun, Moon, Venus, Mars, or Rising Sign: Saturn in Scorpio takes romance quite seriously, as he does every other aspect of his life. This individual will expect you to remain true and faithful to the romance or relationship. You can be assured that having other sexual affairs while involved with Saturn in Scorpio will surely end the relationship. Do not confess or talk about sexual relations with other people, since Scorpio is famous for being jealous and possessive. Scorpio is known for having a highly sexual imagination, but he is seldom promiscuous and doesn't want you to be with anyone else—not in the past and certainly not now or in the future. In past lives, you and your lover with Saturn in Scorpio had a deep and involving romantic affair that ended prematurely or even tragically. Cultures having past-life connections with Scorpio were during the Old Kingdoms of Egypt, the Celtic societies, and the Near Eastern cultures, especially those that are now mainly Islamic.

SATURN IN SAGITTARIUS

For those born from December 1926 through March 1929 or May 1929 through November 1929 or November 1985 through January 1988. The nature of Saturn and the astrological sign of Sagittarius are quite antithetical to each other. Sagittarius wants to expand and enlarge, while Saturn pulls in and limits. Therefore, this Saturn sign contains great contradictions and anxiety. The Saturn-in-Sagittarius individual has a pronounced rebellious streak. He strives for freedom and yearns to break free of his shackles, although freedom is often denied him because of his choices. Saturn in Sagittarius marries late, in a rush, or not at all. At times, this individual is passive-aggressive in his need to rebel and to upset the apple cart. He sabotages the plans of others so as not to be confined by them, let alone be bound by any person or rule. Here we have the "left at the altar scenario" that the rest of the signs have nightmares about. If astrology has "players," Sagittarius is surely the sign that represents them. At times, Saturn in Sagittarius appears rather gentle and holy. This Saturn sign is fascinated with philosophy and religion, going through phases of honoring such traditions and at other times shattering their tenets and rules. In romance, Saturn in Sagittarius is drawn to sojourners and adventurers. Lovers should show a spirit that seeks adventure just like Saturn in Sagittarius.

If Your Lover's Saturn in Sagittarius Connects With Your Sun, Moon, Venus, Mars, or Rising Sign: If you are romantically involved with Saturn in Sagittarius, you can be assured the relationship will not be a typical one. After all, neither Saturn nor Sagittarius are particularly romantic and this is something you will come to accept. Instead, you will become partners in crime and adventure. Conquering new lands and ideas will be at the forefront of your relationship. Romance will be experienced best in thrilling and exotic places, rather than at home. In past lives, you and Saturn in Sagittarius were fellow travelers. Perhaps you were soldiers at war or religious leaders who helped the poor. At any rate, your ideas and beliefs brought you together, as they do now.

SATURN IN CAPRICORN

For those born from December 1929 through February 1932 or January 1956 through December 1958 or November 1988 through January 1991. The Saturn-in-Capricorn lover tends to be reserved and aloof. This sign is a placement of certain harsh karmic lessons. True romance or meeting up with a soulmate will be experienced later in life, if at all. Saturn in Capricorn is terrified of opening up and sharing with others emotionally. Therefore, romantic relationships will take some degree of patience and understanding. Saturn in Capricorn does hold certain faulty beliefs. Individuals born under this sign tend to believe that connecting up with the "right people" (meaning the rich and influential) is the answer to their prayers. They also have a sense of entitlement, striving to improve their social or financial stature through relationships. In other words, they cover the practical angles first; only then can your romance with them flourish. Reaching Saturn in Capricorn emotionally in a close, intimate way can be tough, but it can be accomplished once you win his trust. Also, keep in mind that Saturn here can bring on many moods and bouts of melancholy similar to Saturn in Cancer. This sign is one of ambition and fortitude. If you appreciate the "niceties" of life and wish to improve your status, Saturn in Capricorn is the one to stay close to, as this is one of the most eminently successful Saturn signs of all.

If Your Lover's Saturn in Capricorn Connects With Your Sun, Moon, Venus, Mars, or Rising Sign: Once encouraged, Saturn in Capricorn develops into a patient and gentle lover. This sign desires sex and closeness as much as anyone else, but a physical awkwardness is always apparent. After all, this sign was probably made to feel guilty over sex as a child, which created both anxiety and repression. Despite the inhibitions, Saturn in Capricorn blossoms when given the right amount of romantic attention. Romance with Saturn in Capricorn works best when the lovers have joint interests and similar ambitions. Past-life connections were likely made in northern cultures where food, warmth, and comfort were rare luxuries.

SATURN IN AQUARIUS

For those born from March 1932 through March 1935 or January 1962 through March 1964 or February 1991 through April 1993. This Saturn sign must express his individuality and strives to be different. There are, however, constraints and limitations that somehow stem from childhood and the past. Saturn in Aquarius is an exalted sign, meaning somewhat ennobled, so this indicates a strong individual who is not afraid to stand alone for a cause. The Saturn-in-Aquarius individual connects romantically with a lover who is unique or who stands out in a crowd. Since Saturn-in-Aquarius people are attracted to the arts, especially functional kinds of art, artists are people they easily connect with. Romantically, they seek the varied and the unusual. They tend to go where people follow their impulses and souls, no matter how strange or taboo this may seem to others. Members of their families may be surprised or even horrified. Bisexuality is one aspect of the Saturn-in-Aquarius individual but they go through many attractions. Above all else, Saturn in Aquarius people try to break free of anything that will inhibit them and their desire to explore the new and different.

If Your Lover's Saturn in Aquarius Connects With Your Sun, Moon, Venus, Mars, or Rising Sign: As lovers, you work best toward a cause that is larger than both of you. Romance should be exciting and varied. Your romance will involve other people, most of whom are your Saturn in Aquarius' friends and associates. You will be encouraged to be different and experimental, but within the framework of a group or a clique. Sex will be greatly exciting, bordering on the taboo or weird. Be careful not to sink into entropy, as Aquarius sometimes allows reality to slip away into something kinky, well beyond ordinary sexual tastes. When you are with a Saturn-in-Aquarius lover, expect the unexpected and get used to the jolts and shocks. Past-life connections may have been in Asia, Atlantis, Guatemala, and even outer space. When properly grounded, Saturn in Aquarius will carry you to the stars where not even the sky is the limit!

SATURN IN PISCES

For those born from March 1935 through April 1937 or April 1964 through February 1967 or May 1993 through March 1996. This is another moody, melancholy Saturn sign. These people feel deeply and are sensitive to vibes and all kinds of impressions that float through the air, both positive and negative. Throughout their lives, Saturn-in-Pisces people feel abandoned or abused and so make themselves into martyrs. Everyone who surrounds Saturn-in-Pisces people gets involved in their drama. Fascinated by all spiritual matters, they are especially interested in the psychic world and other realms. To manage a lover with Saturn in Pisces, be forewarned to expect many crisis-and-rescue cycles and this can be tiring. After all, Pisceans need to be pointed in the right direction. There are so many to choose from, Pisces stays confused! Never underestimate the powers of this beautiful sign. They are charismatic, much in the way that Scorpio is. Pisceans have the power; they just don't realize that they do. Pisces needs a manager and a person who doesn't mind setting his life straight. Saturn in Pisces has much to give the world, but he needs help and assistance in giving it. Persons born under this sign just don't know how much they are worth!

If Your Lover's Saturn in Pisces Connects With Your Sun, Moon, Venus, Mars, or Rising Sign: Individuals with Saturn in

Pisces seek sexual fulfillment but believe they must be punished for their sins. They are often attracted to people who are rather severe or punitive; they see this as strong. This can be a problem, of course. If your lover or you has Saturn in Pisces, and there is a connection, you can be assured that both of you suffered for a cause in past lives. Your past lives are connected to peoples such as the Persians, the early Christians, the Minoans, or those living in the Far East.

Saturn signs in your horoscope represent how you and your lover are bound to each other despite obstacles, distances, or any frustrations that are placed in your way. This gorgeous rainbow planet, which inspires both dread and awe among astrologers, also represents an everlasting tie between two people. If your natal Saturn sign and that of your lover somehow connect, expect this love affair to be immortal. This is surely a romance that will either send both of you to hell or carry you high into heaven. Through patience, toil, and some strong effort, you were born to be together for you have surely met the lover of your dreams.

CONCLUSION:
MAKING LOVE LAST

So after the sex, what comes next? Without that sexual spark, love relationships will undoubtedly wither. The same is true of relationships between lovers who have nothing in common except for the sex. The highs of perfect sex intoxicate our hearts and our minds, but such sudden attractions tend not to last too long.

Many famous romances were based on sexual chemistry as is spelled out in the stars, but many of those famous romances also ended. We remember them, perhaps, for their passion. We forget about the disappointment if the romance didn't continue. Still, we want the fairy tale. We need the myth. The conventions of our culture tells us this is what we need to be happy.

Love lasts only if some truth inside of you says that you and your lover will go on, that there is permanence to your love. As long as you are willing to work together as two hearts, two minds, and two souls toward a common goal, love will last. Don't expect sex to be the most important bond. If the sex is great, but you are neither respected or understood, obviously the sex will lose its glamour and each of you will go your separate ways.

The same is true of our own lives, where we go from relationship to relationship in a series of disappointing cycles searching for the *perfect* one. No, your prince or princess won't come, and you can't force him or her to. Your prince or princess probably doesn't exist. The Emperor doesn't have any clothes on, either.

Yet you can meet your lover in some place of understanding by spelling out what it is you need, what you stand for, and who you really are. After all, your ideal lover is merely an imperfect human like yourself.

As Shakespeare once wrote, our fates lie not in the stars but in ourselves. I differ with this sentiment only slightly, by saying that our fates lie both in our stars and in our selves. Yet the stars can guide us in understanding *clearly* who we are, and in the end, it is through the stars that we can know our lovers as well as we know ourselves.